THE GREATEST EVER JEWISH CARTOON BOO

Also by Neil Kerber

The Great Jewish Cartoon Book

THE GREATEST EVER JEWISH CARTOON BOOK

Neil Kerber

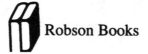

Robson Books

First published in Great Britain in 2001 by Robson Books
64 Brewery Road, London N7 9NY

A member of the Chrysalis Group plc

British Library Cataloguing in Publication Data
A catalogue record for this title is available from the British Library.

ISBN 186105438 6

Typeset by FiSH Books, London WC1
Printed by St Edmundsbury Press, Bury St Edmunds, suffolk

In memory of Brian
who died this year.

A truly great cat.

Acknowledgements

To mum and dad,
Richard and Merryl,
and Kerbers everywhere.

To David Black
who isn't quite as funny as me,
but tries hard.
And to Sue and Alfie.

Thank you Amy
for putting up with me
during the making of
this great epic.

Thanks also to the
Jewish Chronicle for
publishing my Jewish stuff.

This book is dedicated to
Rose, Joe and Emma.
xxx

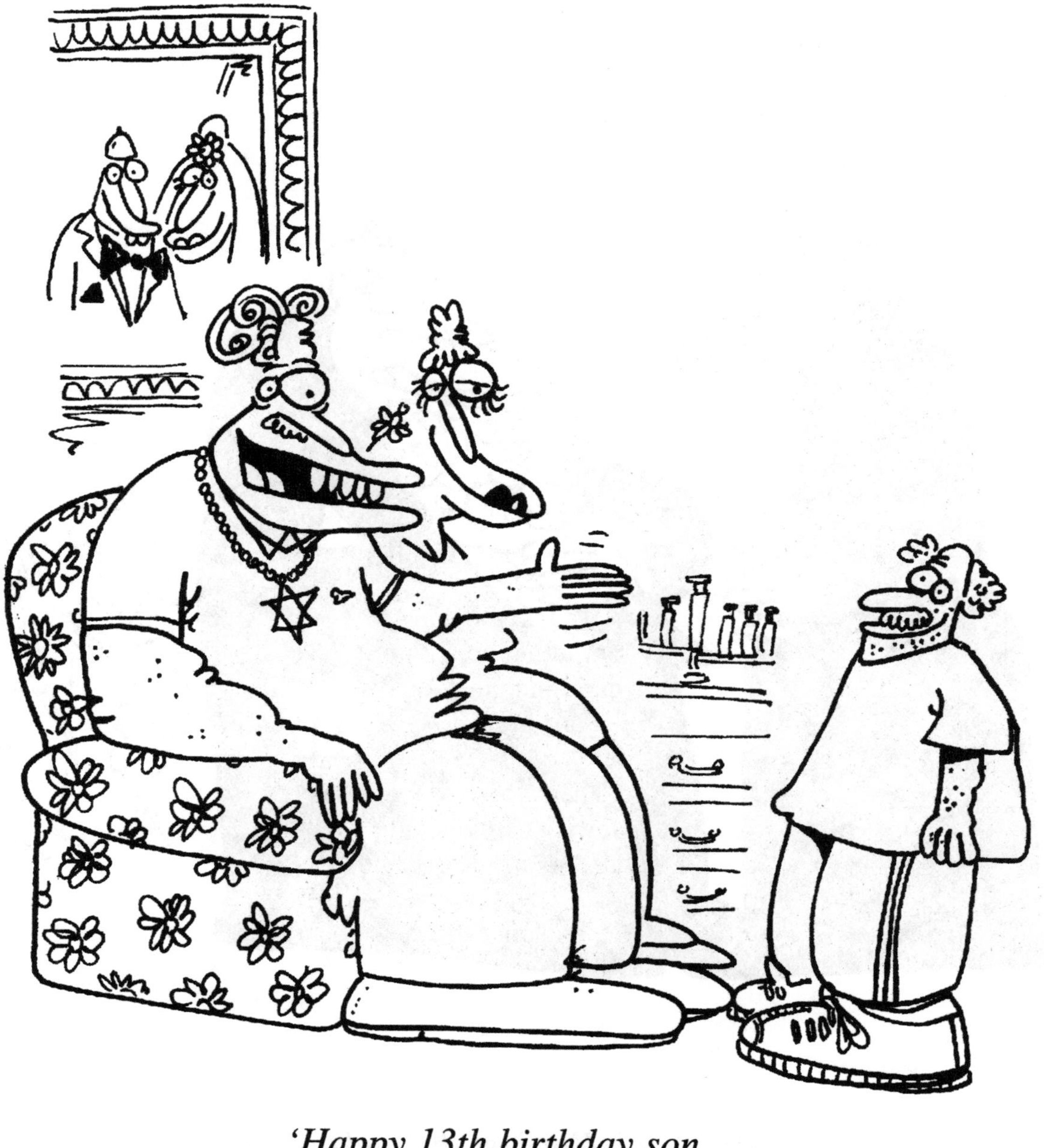

*'Happy 13th birthday son.
Now you're a man!'*

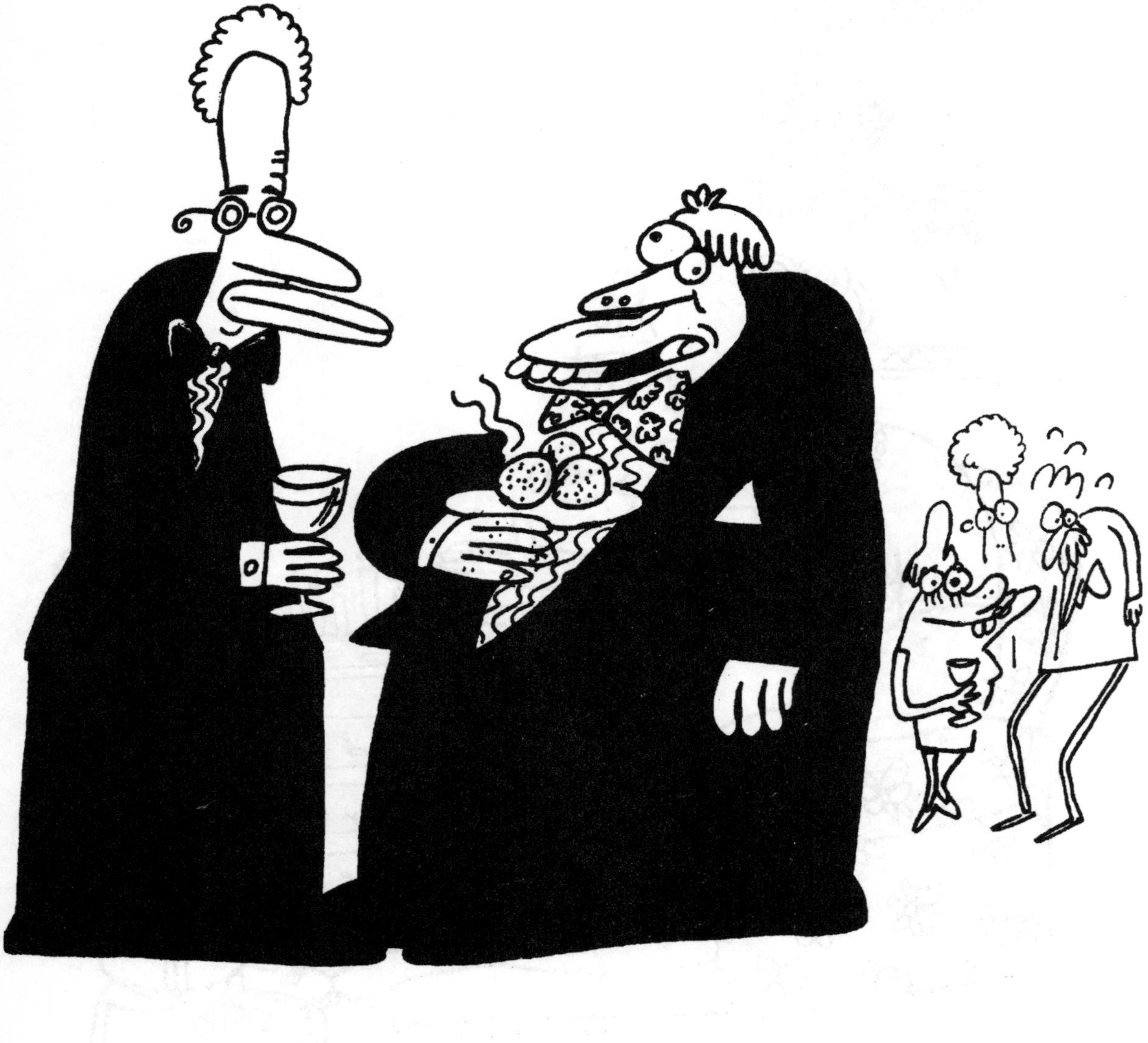

'Me?...oh I'm just the awkard guy you always get stuck with at Jewish weddings!'

THE CHOSEN EPISODE 1

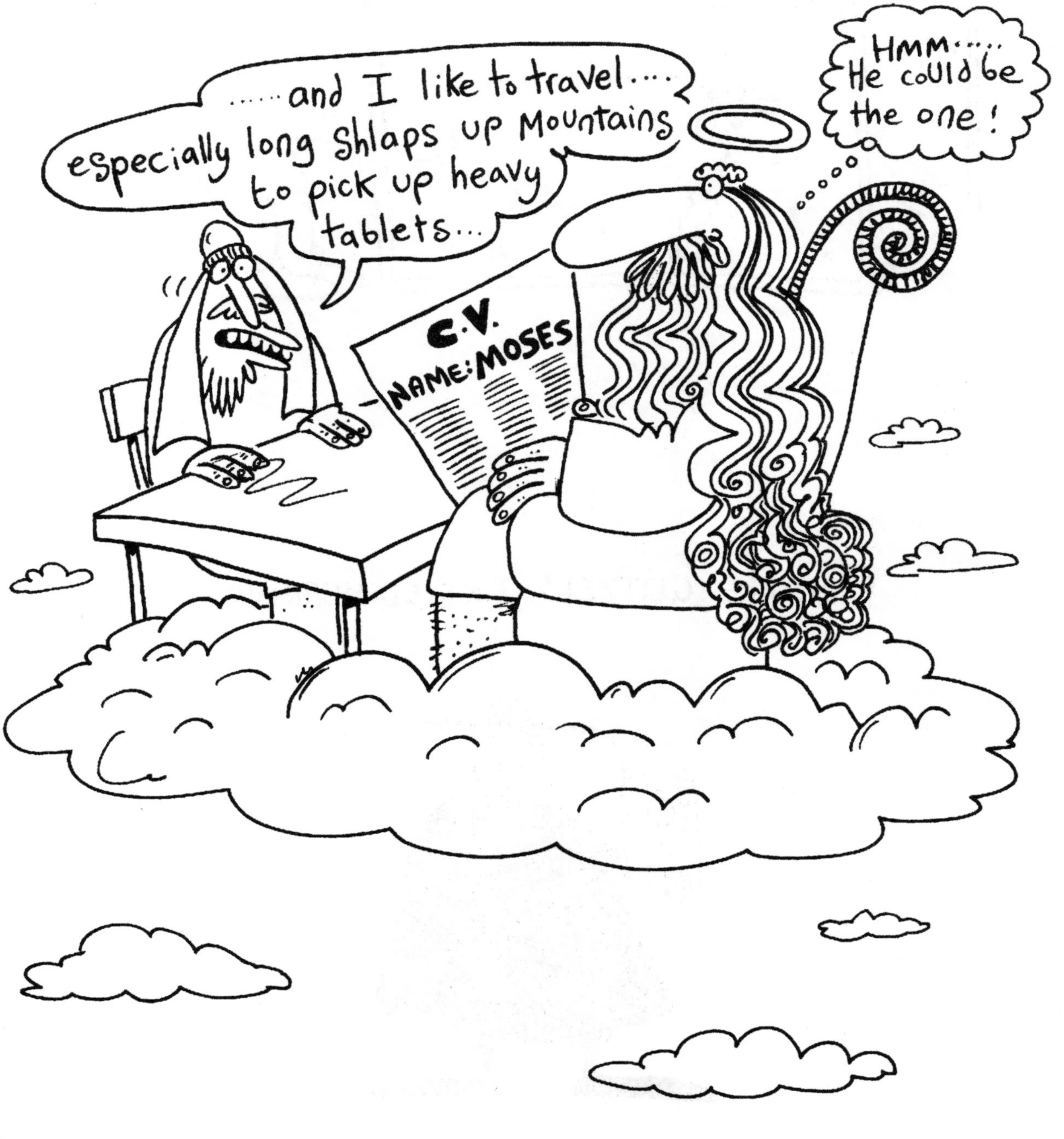
......and I like to travel.... especially long shlaps up Mountains to pick up heavy tablets...
HMM..... He could be the one!
C.V. NAME: MOSES

Contraversial Modern Art

DAMIEN HIRST'S PICKLED SHEEP:

SHLOYMIE GLITZEL'S PICKLED HERRING:

A Passover tale

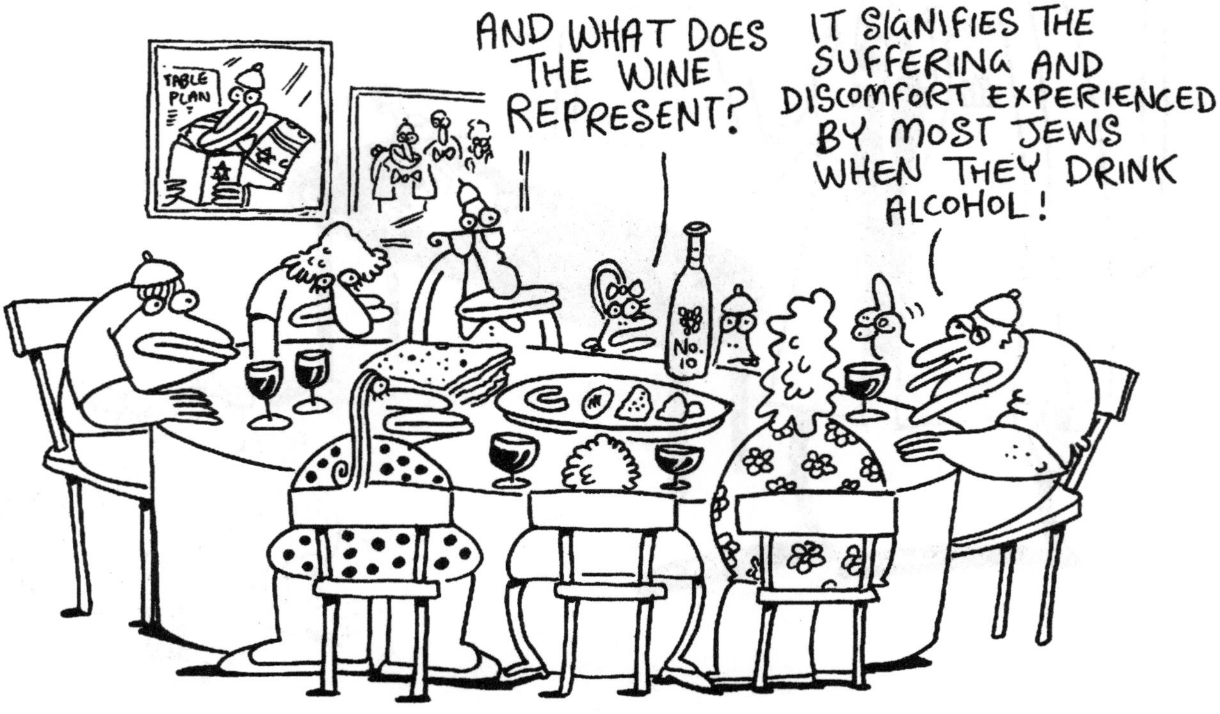

TABLE PLAN
AND WHAT DOES THE WINE REPRESENT?
IT SIGNIFIES THE SUFFERING AND DISCOMFORT EXPERIENCED BY MOST JEWS WHEN THEY DRINK ALCOHOL!
No. 10

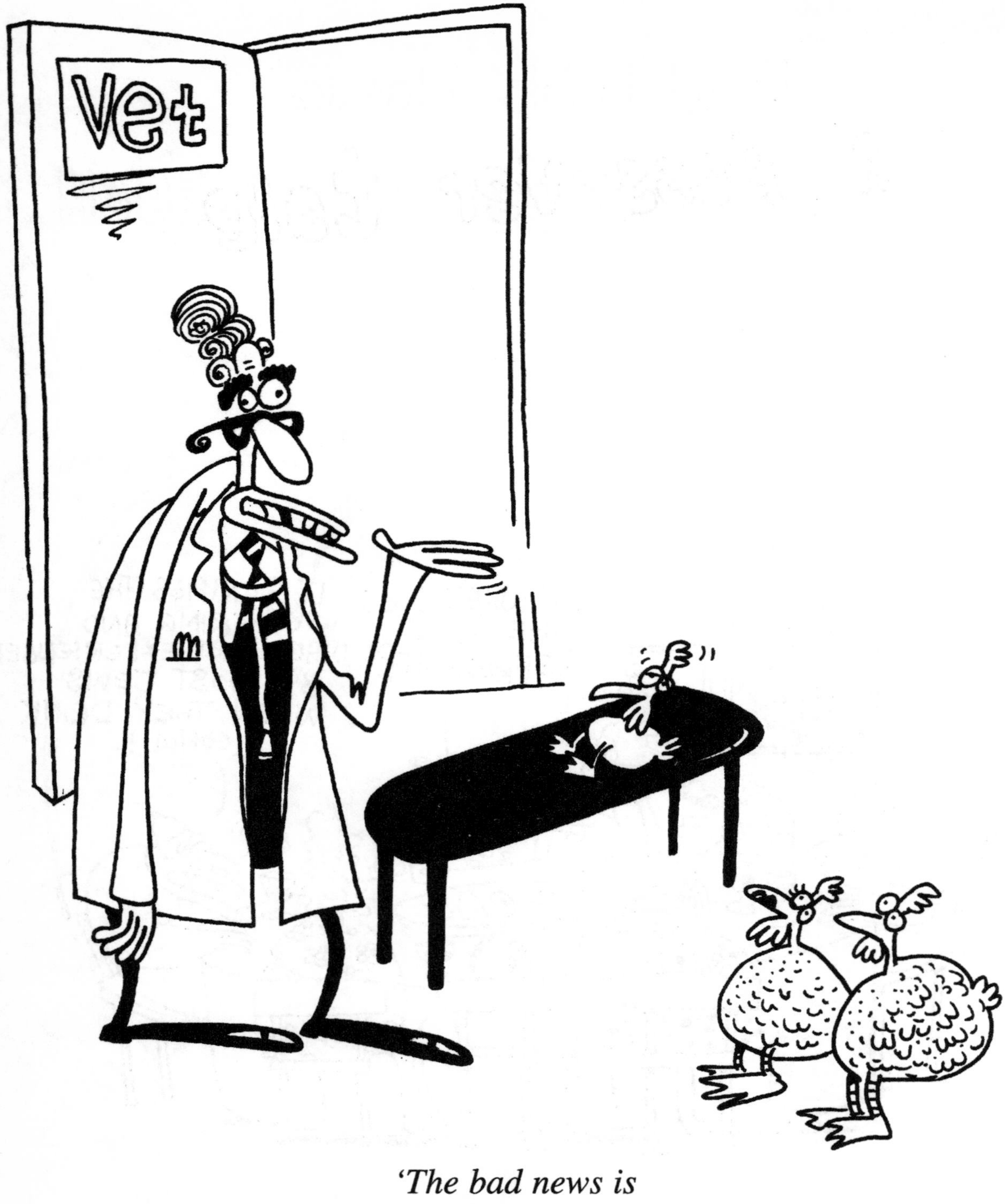

vet

'The bad news is
your son has swallowed a food blender...
The good news is
that we can all have chopped liver!'

From Roald Dahls' classic

YENTA AND THE GIANT PEACH

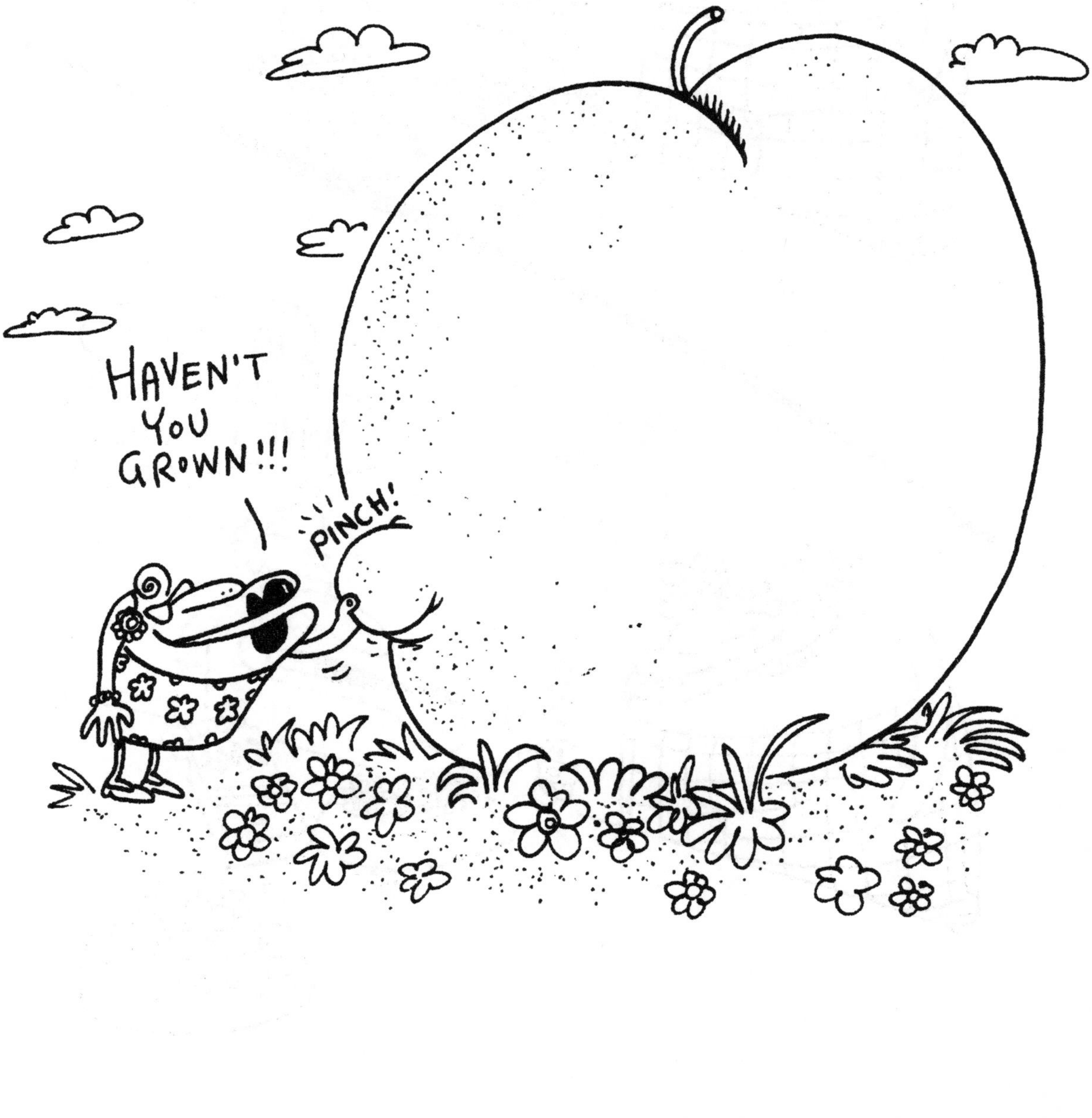
HAVEN'T YOU GROWN!!!
PINCH!

A Jewish New Year's Resolution.....

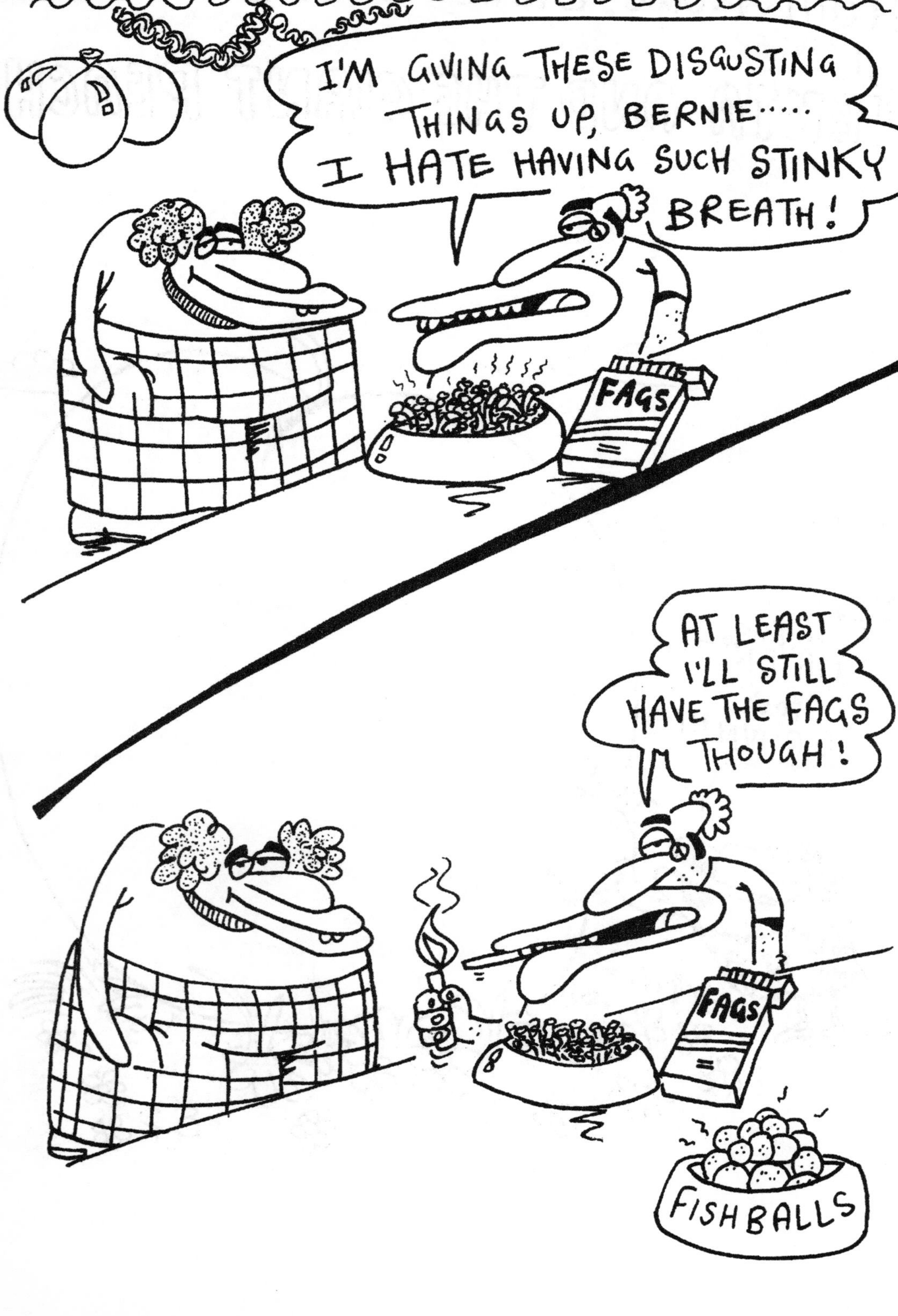
I'M GIVING THESE DISGUSTING THINGS UP, BERNIE..... I HATE HAVING SUCH STINKY BREATH!
FAGS
AT LEAST I'LL STILL HAVE THE FAGS THOUGH!
FAGS
FISHBALLS

THE CHOSEN EPISODE 2

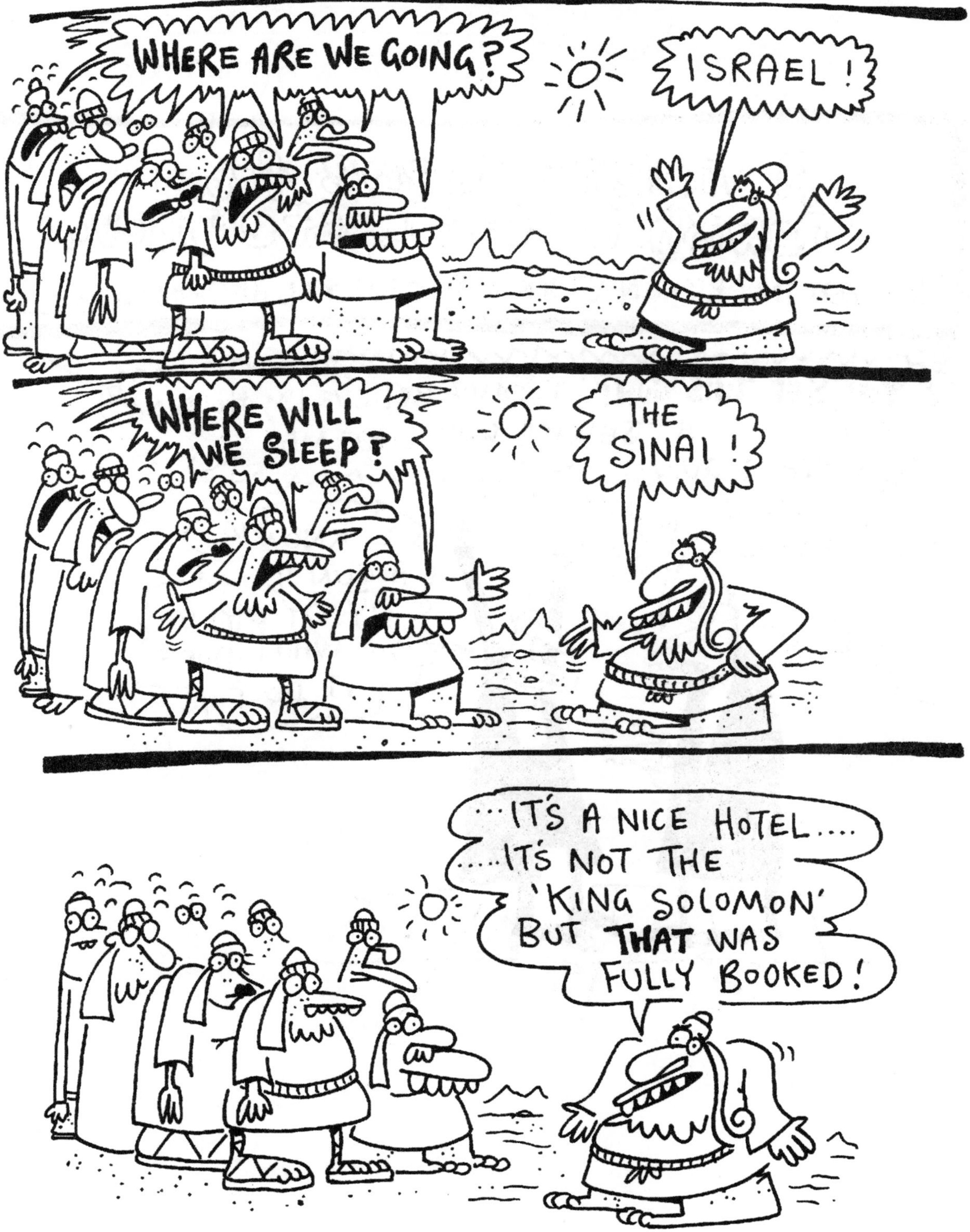
WHERE ARE WE GOING?
ISRAEL!
WHERE WILL WE SLEEP?
THE SINAI!
...IT'S A NICE HOTEL....
....IT'S NOT THE 'KING SOLOMON' BUT THAT WAS FULLY BOOKED!

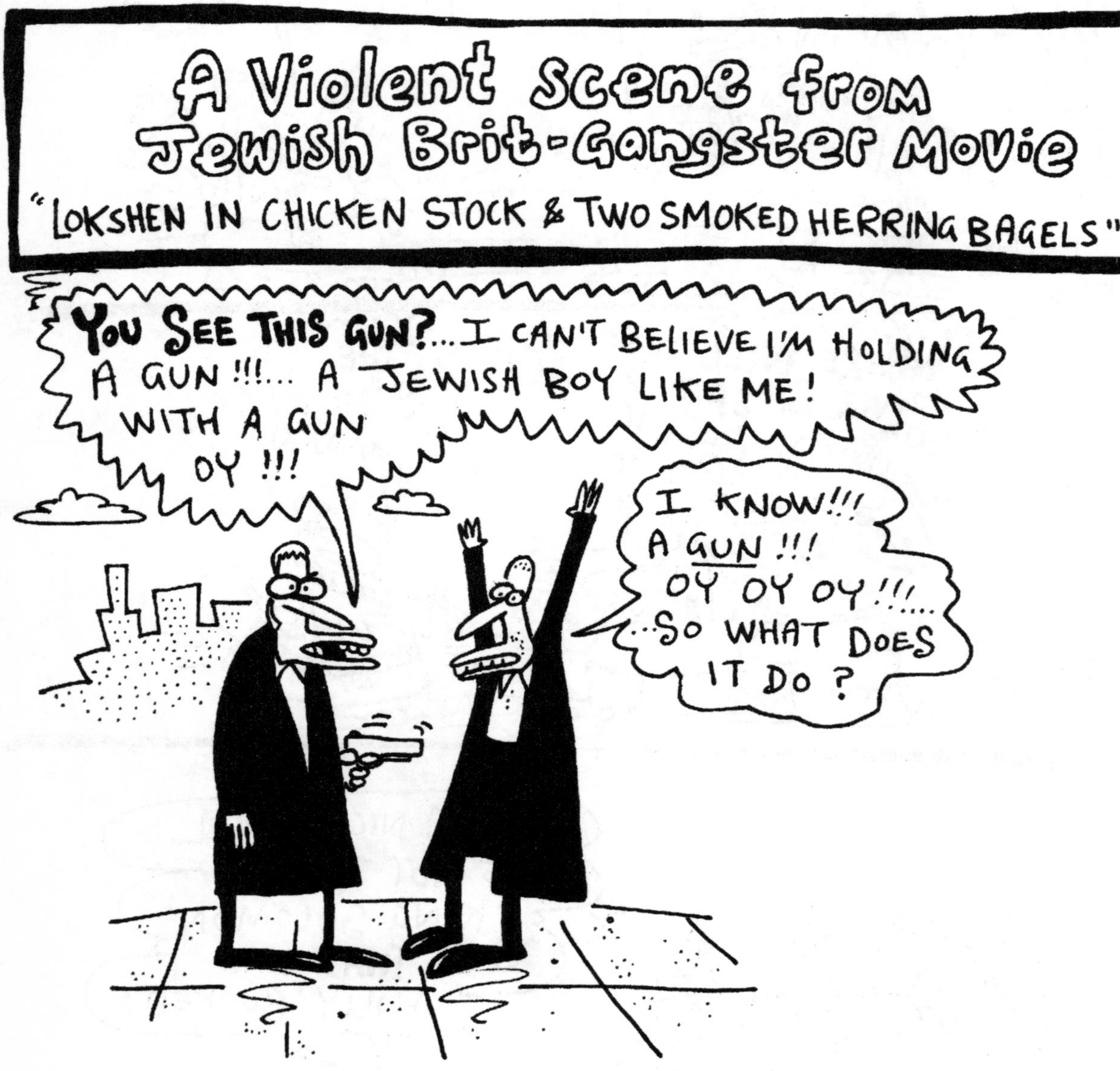
A Violent Scene from Jewish Brit-Gangster Movie
"LOKSHEN IN CHICKEN STOCK & TWO SMOKED HERRING BAGELS"
YOU SEE THIS GUN?... I CAN'T BELIEVE I'M HOLDING A GUN !!!... A JEWISH BOY LIKE ME! WITH A GUN OY !!!
I KNOW!!! A GUN !!! OY OY OY !!!.... ...SO WHAT DOES IT DO ?

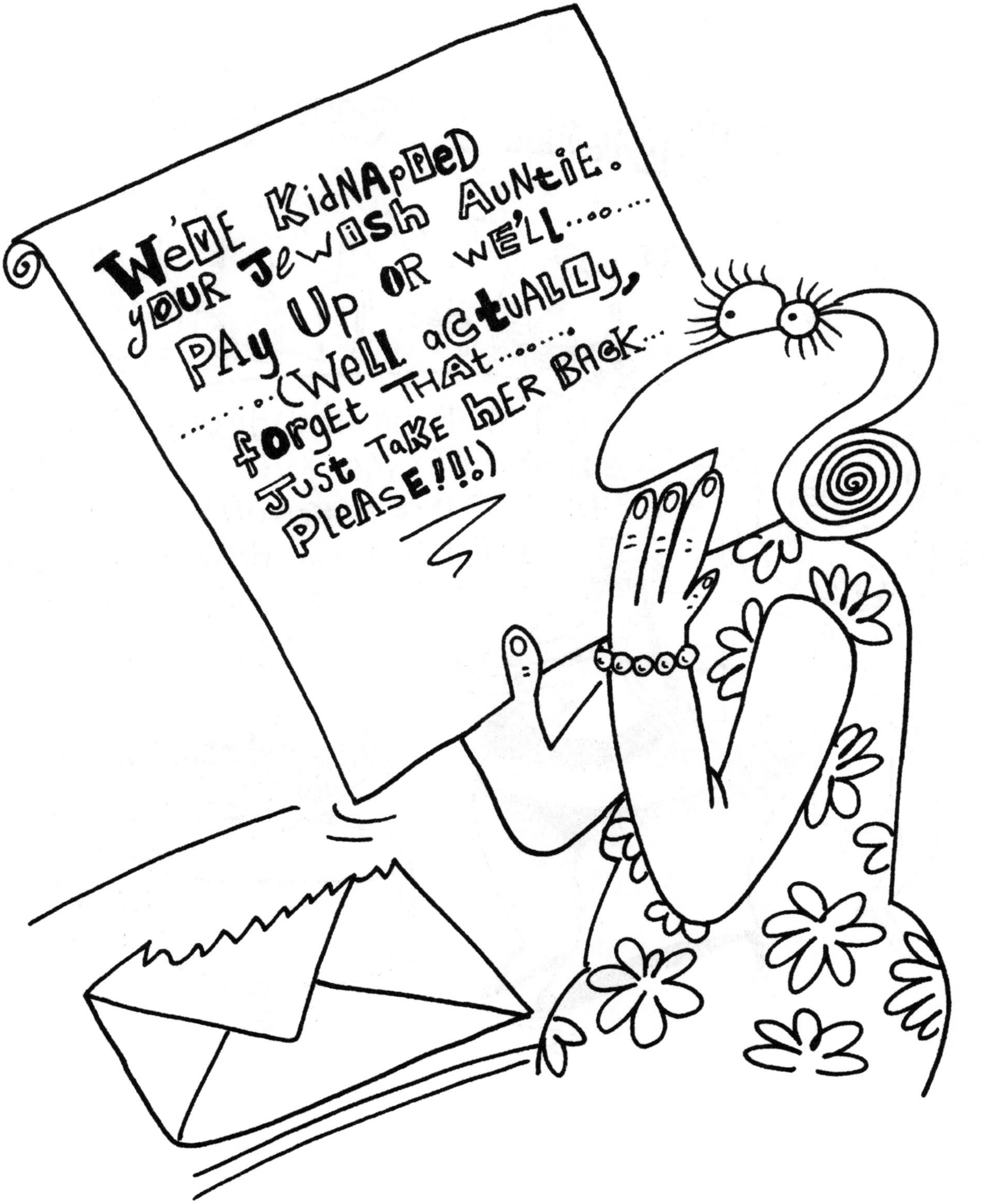
WE'VE KIDNAPPED
YOUR JEWISH AUNTIE.
PAY UP OR WE'LL......
(WELL ACTUALLY,
FORGET THAT.......
JUST TAKE HER BACK...
PLEASE!!!)

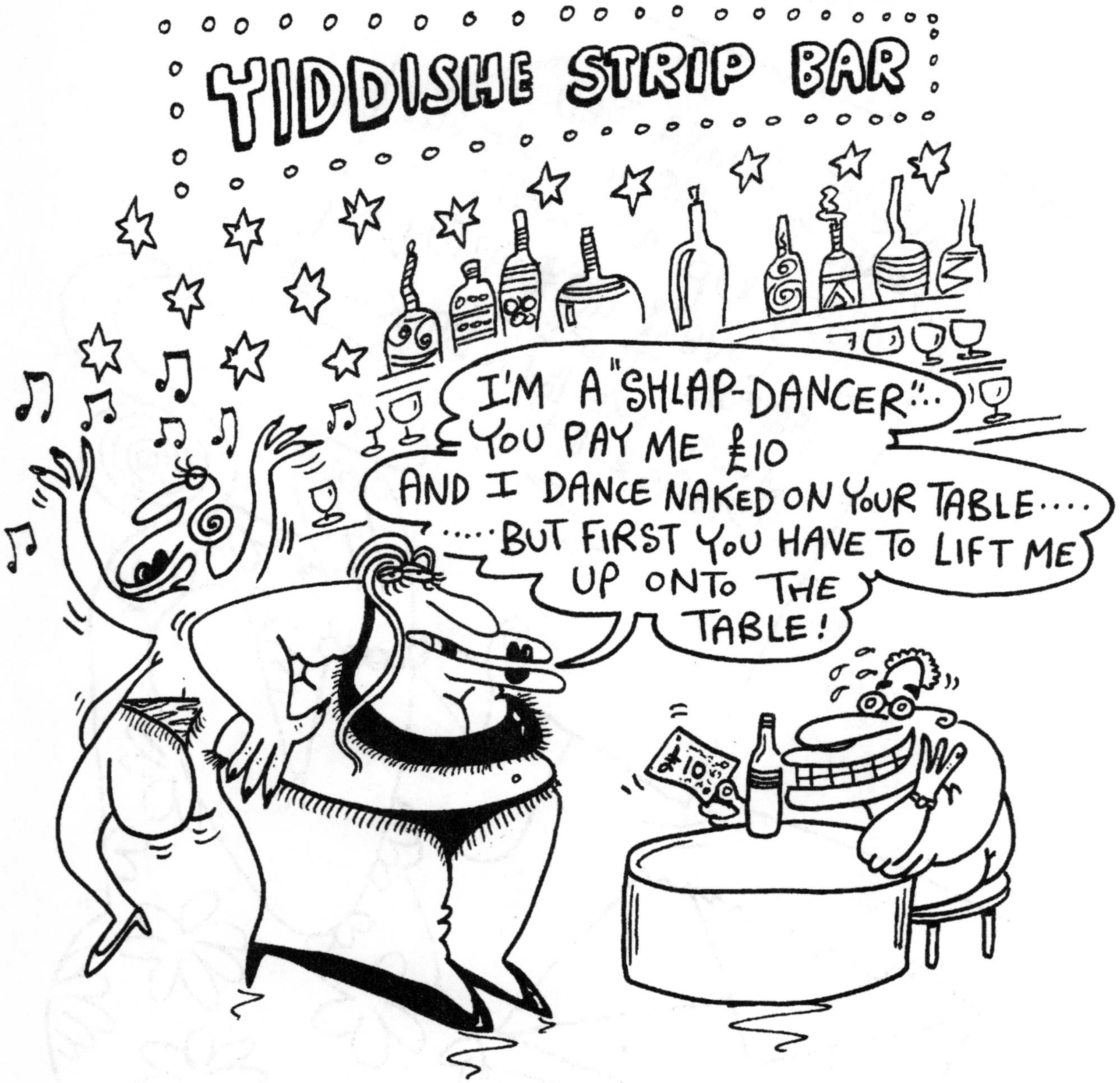

YIDDISHE STRIP BAR
I'M A "SHLAP-DANCER"... YOU PAY ME £10 AND I DANCE NAKED ON YOUR TABLE.... .....BUT FIRST YOU HAVE TO LIFT ME UP ONTO THE TABLE!
£10

DODGY JEWS

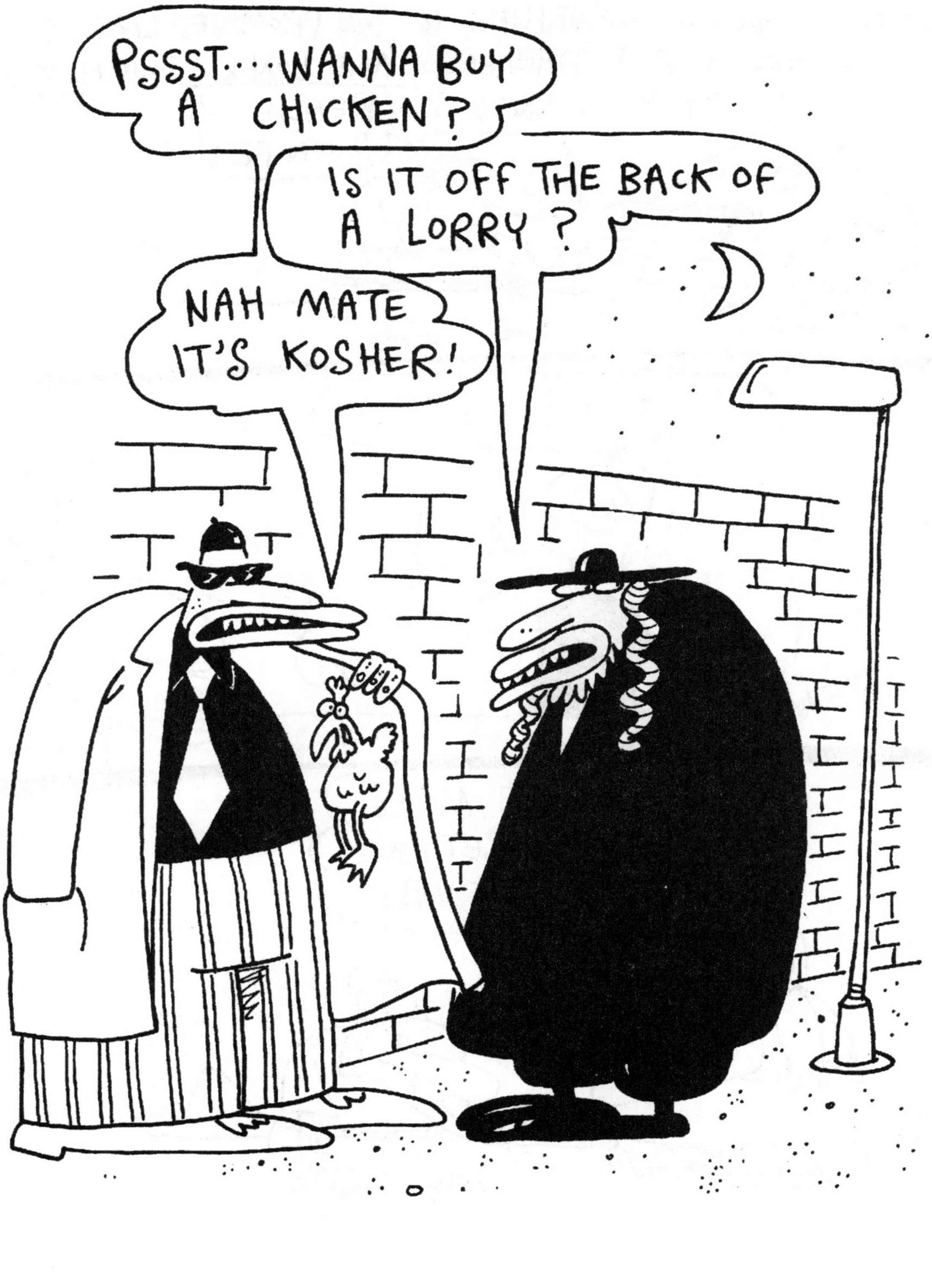
PSSST....WANNA BUY A CHICKEN?
IS IT OFF THE BACK OF A LORRY?
NAH MATE IT'S KOSHER!

THE CHOSEN Episode 3

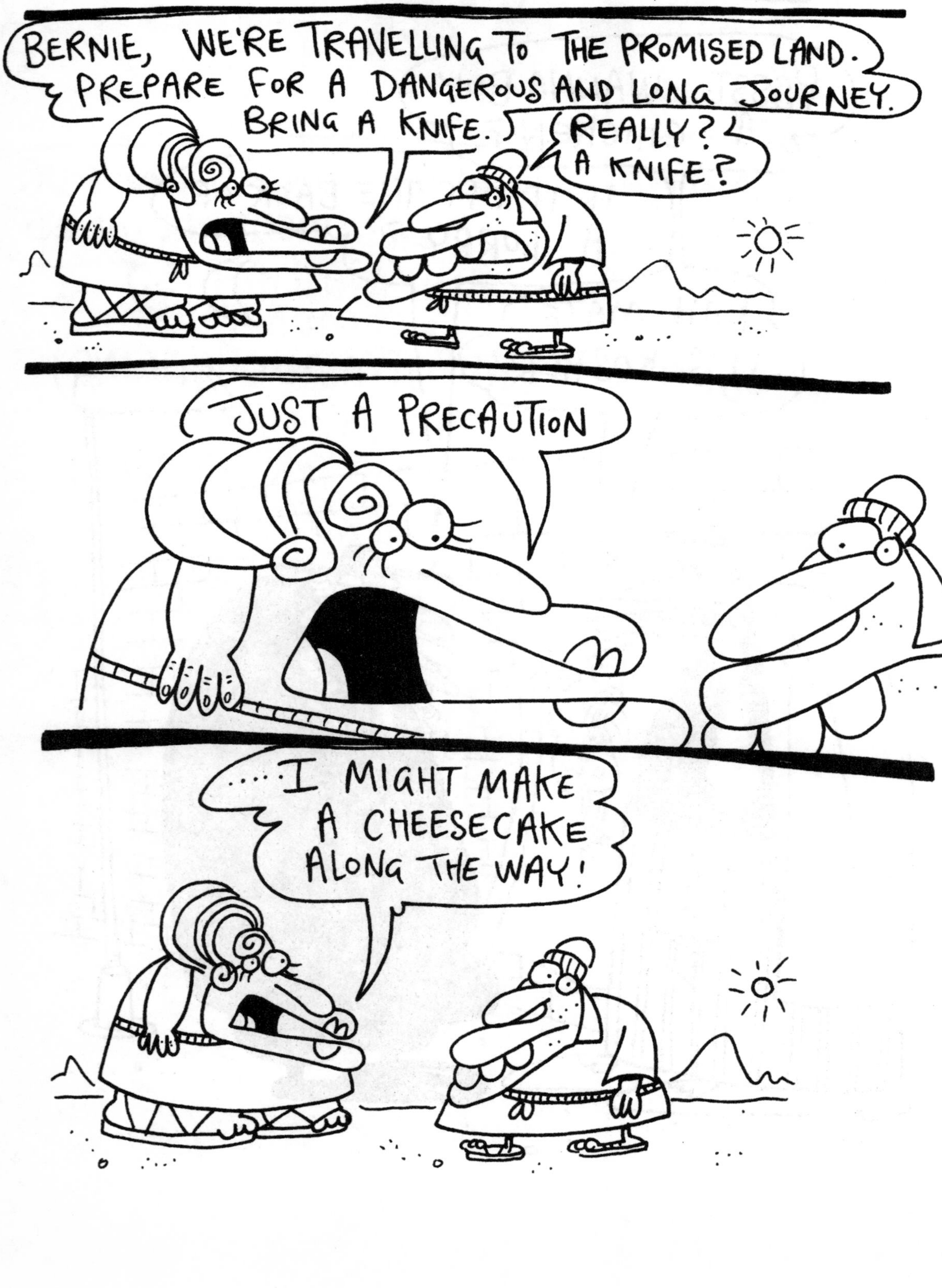
BERNIE, WE'RE TRAVELLING TO THE PROMISED LAND. PREPARE FOR A DANGEROUS AND LONG JOURNEY. BRING A KNIFE.
REALLY? A KNIFE?
JUST A PRECAUTION
....I MIGHT MAKE A CHEESECAKE ALONG THE WAY!

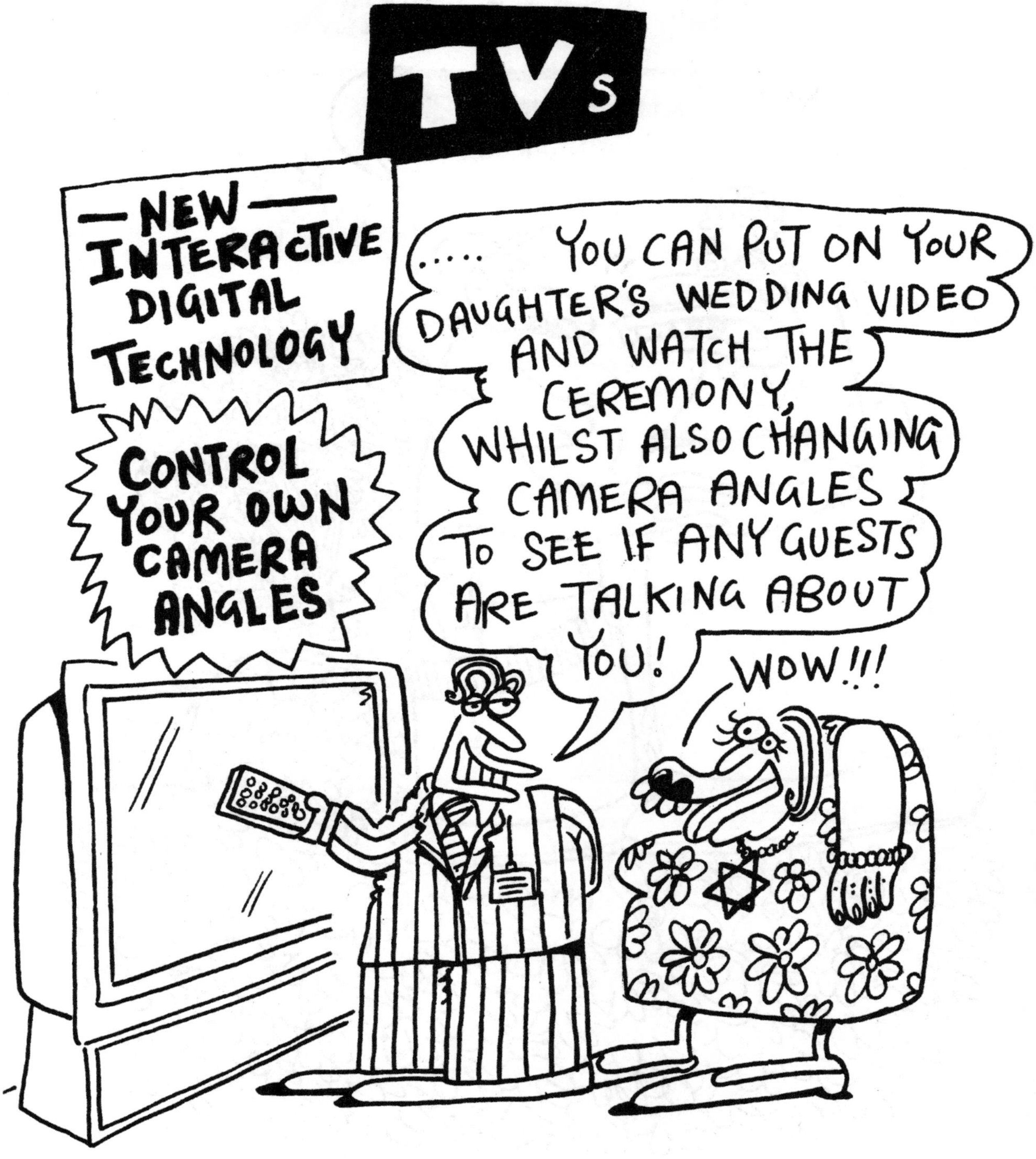
TVs
— NEW — INTERACTIVE DIGITAL TECHNOLOGY
CONTROL YOUR OWN CAMERA ANGLES
..... YOU CAN PUT ON YOUR DAUGHTER'S WEDDING VIDEO AND WATCH THE CEREMONY, WHILST ALSO CHANGING CAMERA ANGLES TO SEE IF ANY GUESTS ARE TALKING ABOUT YOU!
WOW!!!

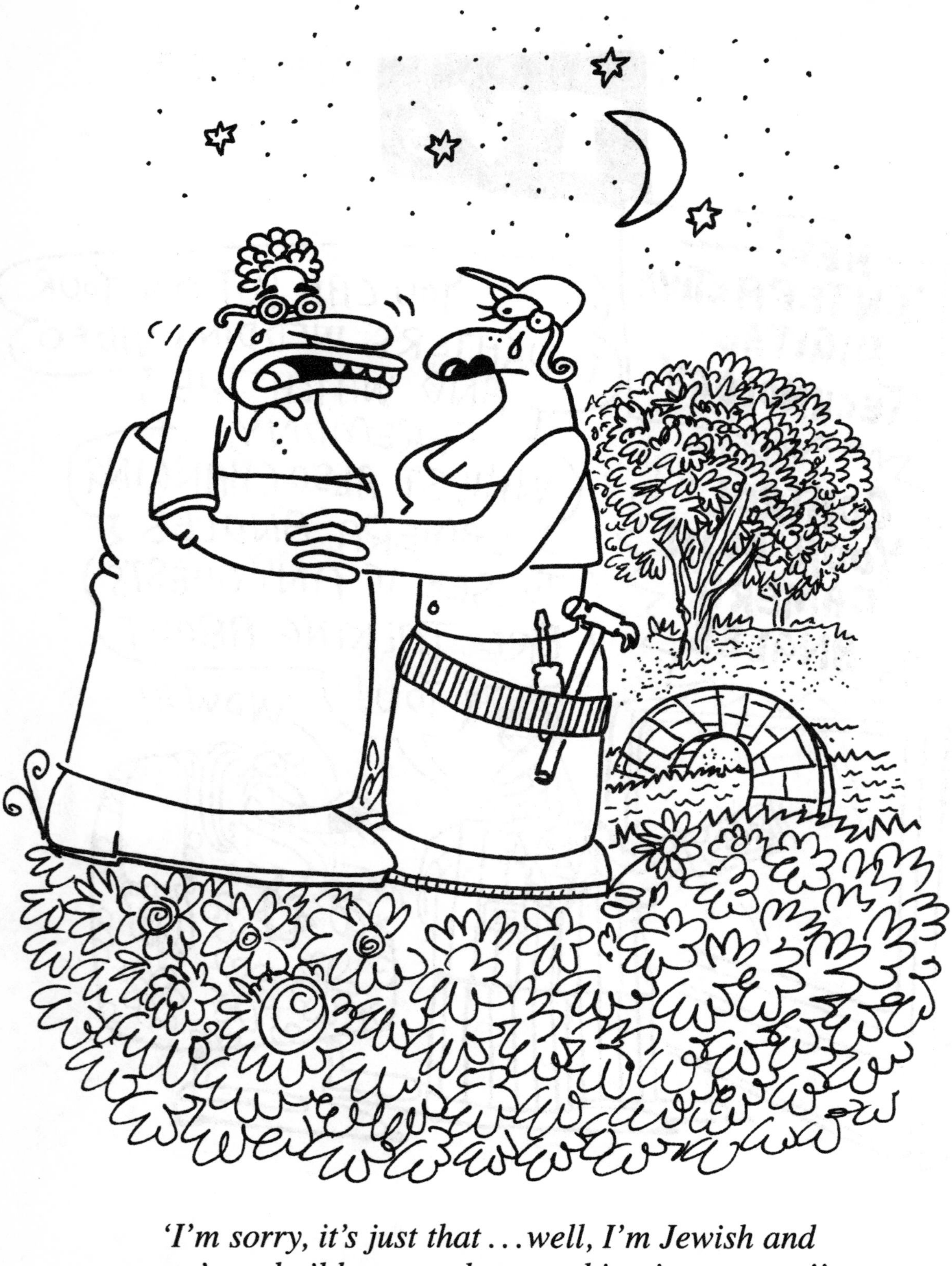

'I'm sorry, it's just that . . . well, I'm Jewish and you're a builder . . . we have nothing in common!'

Cannibal Jewish mothers.......

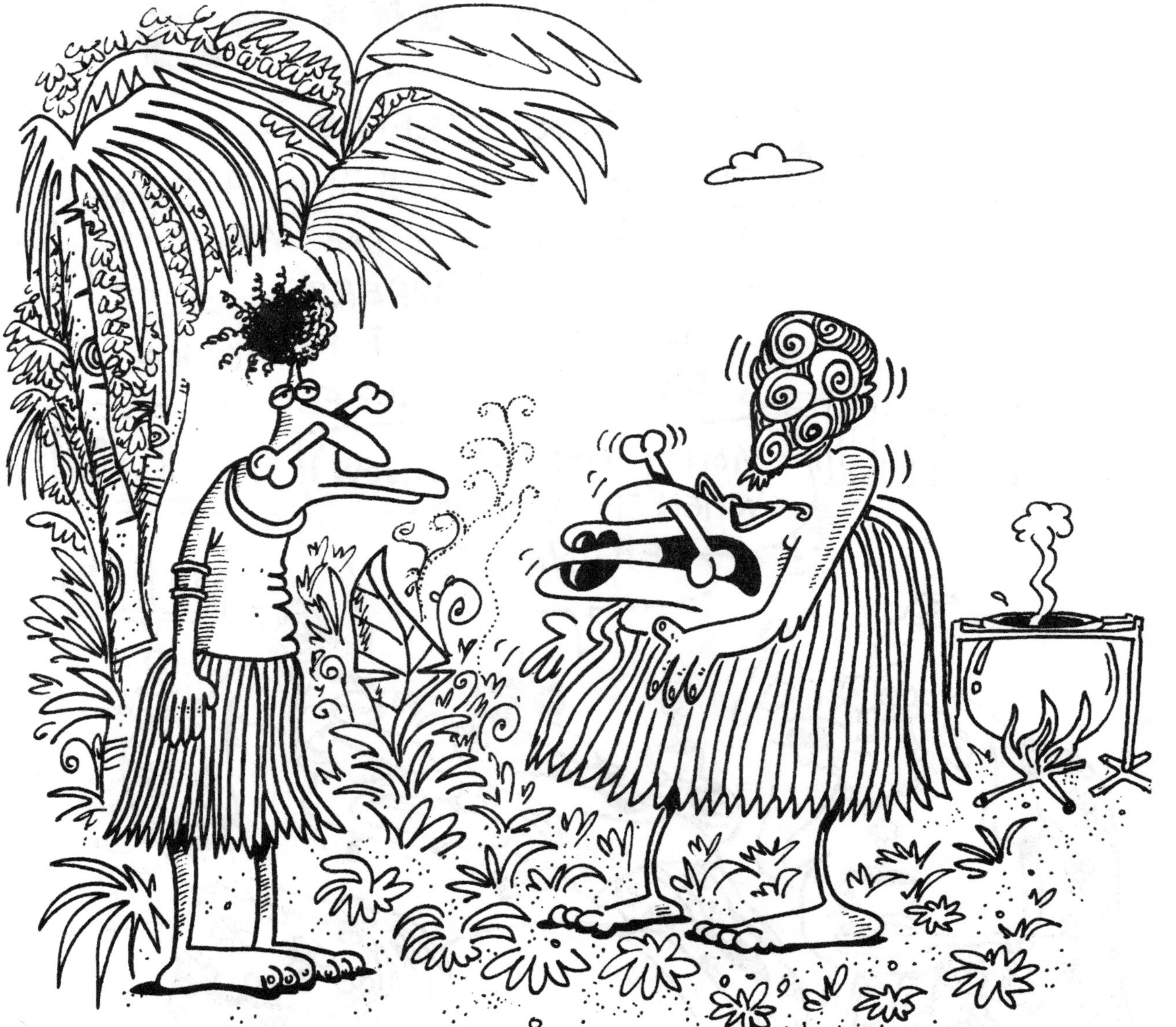

*'Look at you . . . you look so thin . . .
you should eat me!!!'*

The Full Monty

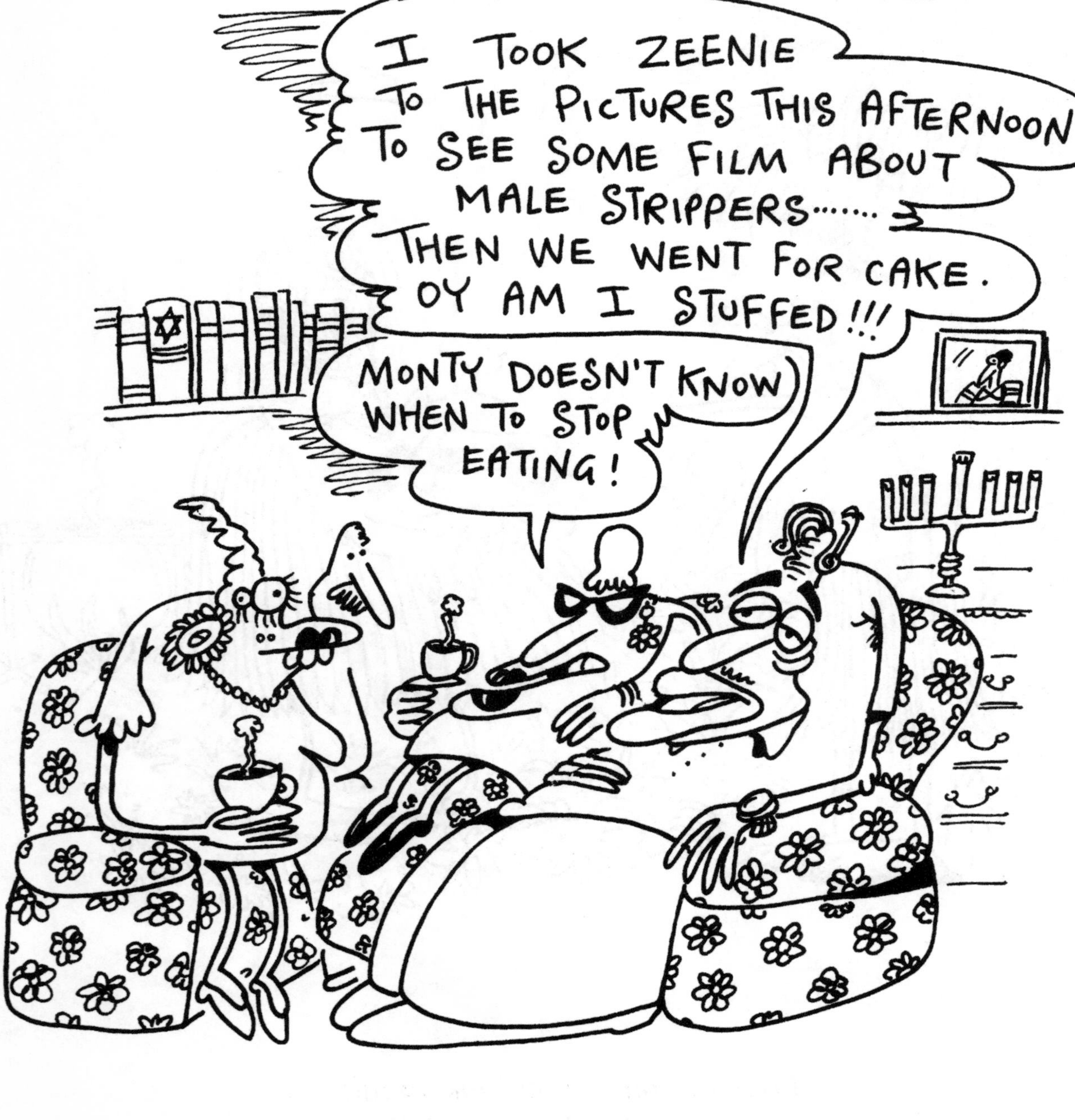
I TOOK ZEENIE TO THE PICTURES THIS AFTERNOON TO SEE SOME FILM ABOUT MALE STRIPPERS....... THEN WE WENT FOR CAKE. OY AM I STUFFED!!!
MONTY DOESN'T KNOW WHEN TO STOP EATING!

Yiddishe 'Ladies of the Night'

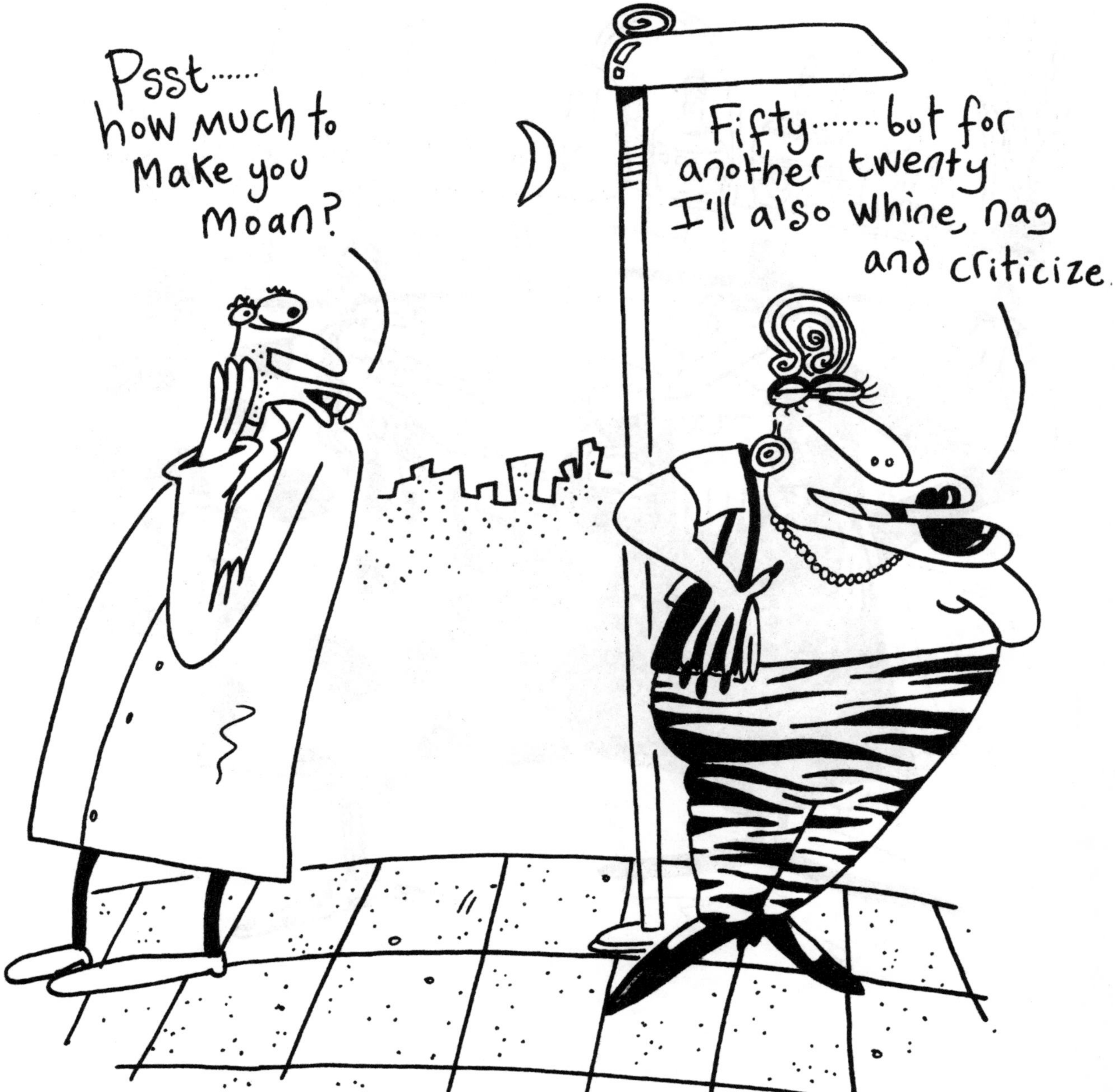
Psst...... how much to make you moan?
Fifty...... but for another twenty I'll also whine, nag and criticize.

'IT' HASSIDICS

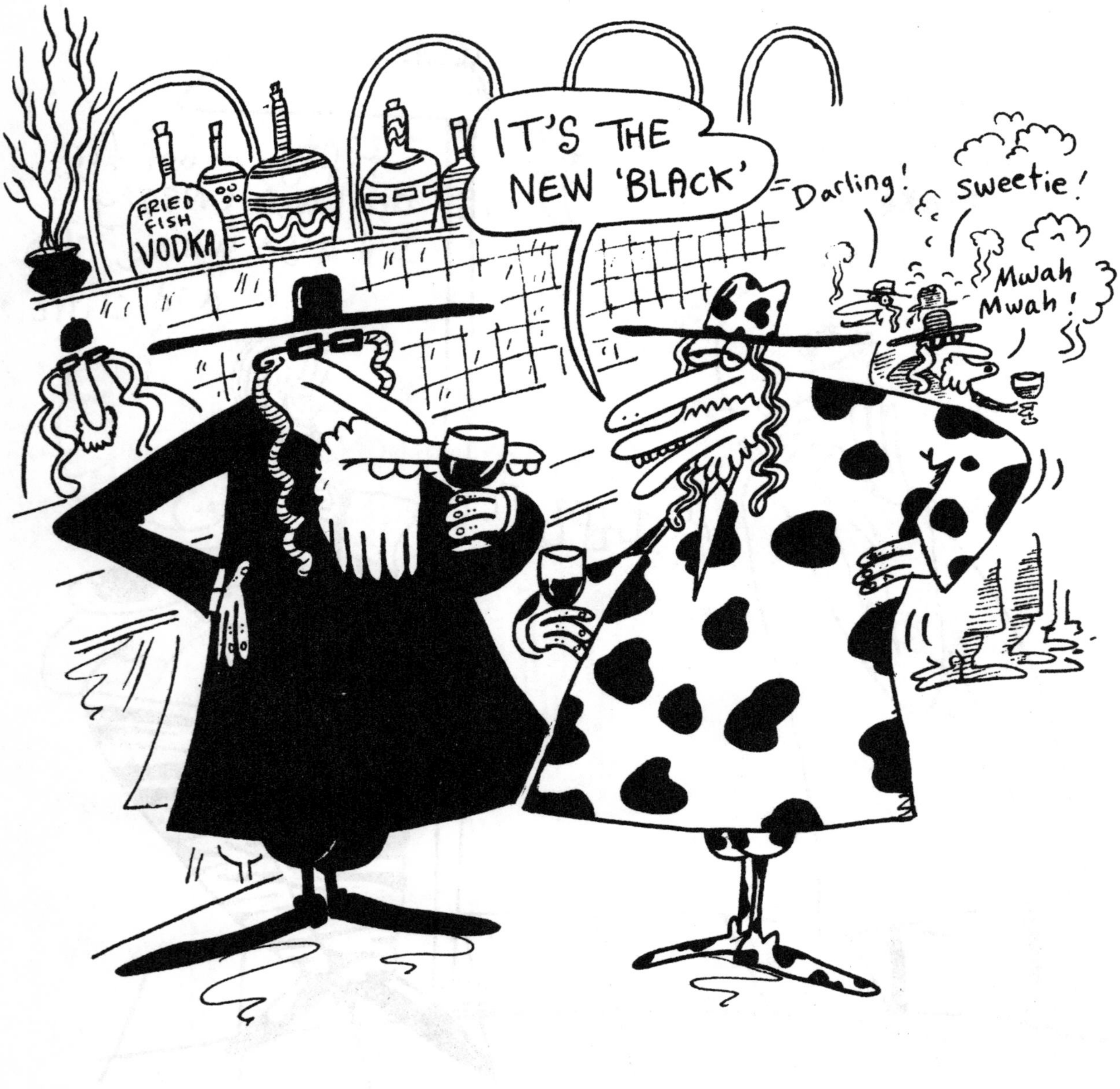

FRIED FISH VODKA
IT'S THE NEW 'BLACK'
Darling!
Sweetie!
Mwah Mwah!

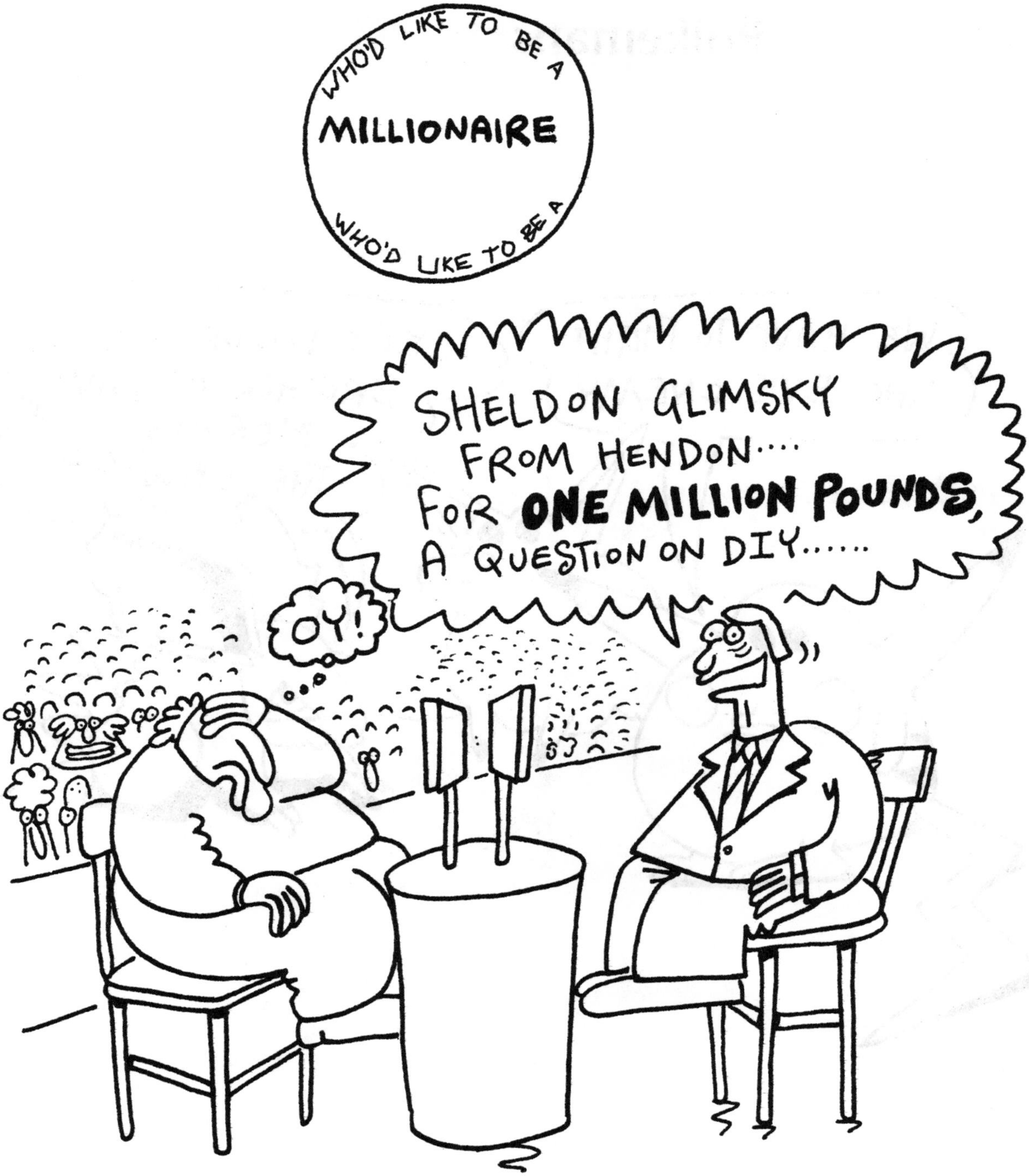
WHO'D LIKE TO BE A
MILLIONAIRE
WHO'D LIKE TO BE A
SHELDON GLIMSKY FROM HENDON.... FOR ONE MILLION POUNDS, A QUESTION ON DIY......
OY!

THE
Polkemans

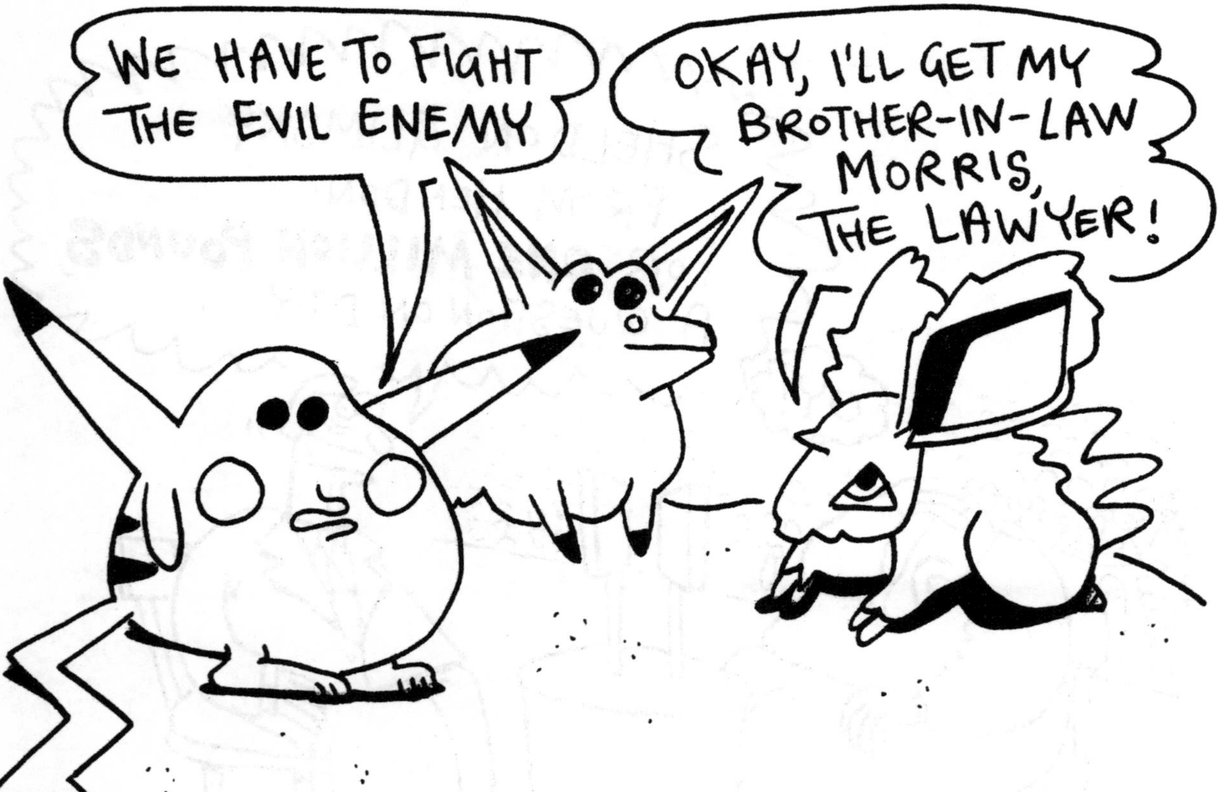
WE HAVE TO FIGHT THE EVIL ENEMY
OKAY, I'LL GET MY BROTHER-IN-LAW MORRIS, THE LAWYER!

THE CHOSEN — EPISODE 4

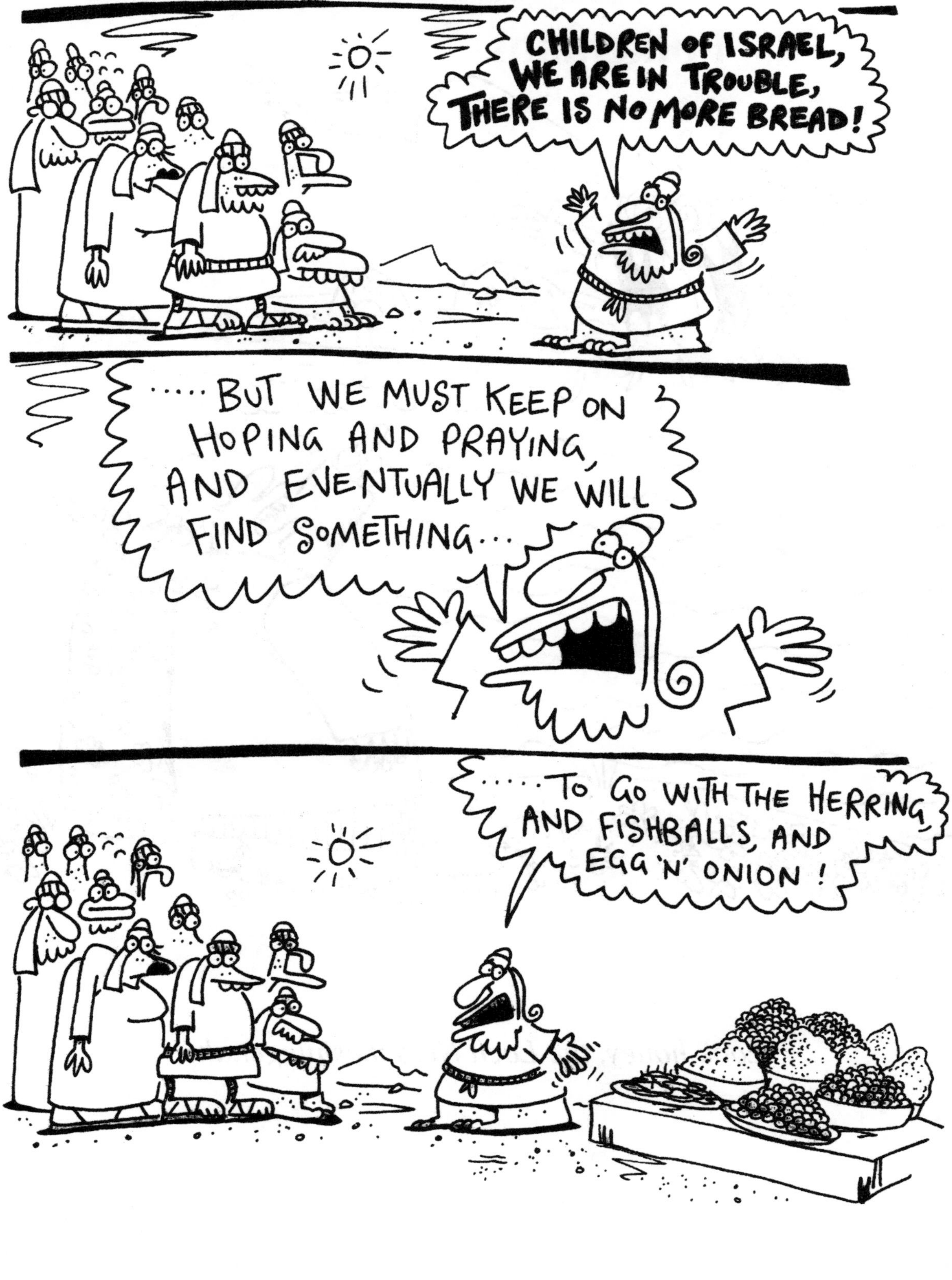
CHILDREN OF ISRAEL, WE ARE IN TROUBLE, THERE IS NO MORE BREAD!
.....BUT WE MUST KEEP ON HOPING AND PRAYING, AND EVENTUALLY WE WILL FIND SOMETHING...
.....TO GO WITH THE HERRING AND FISHBALLS, AND EGG 'N' ONION!

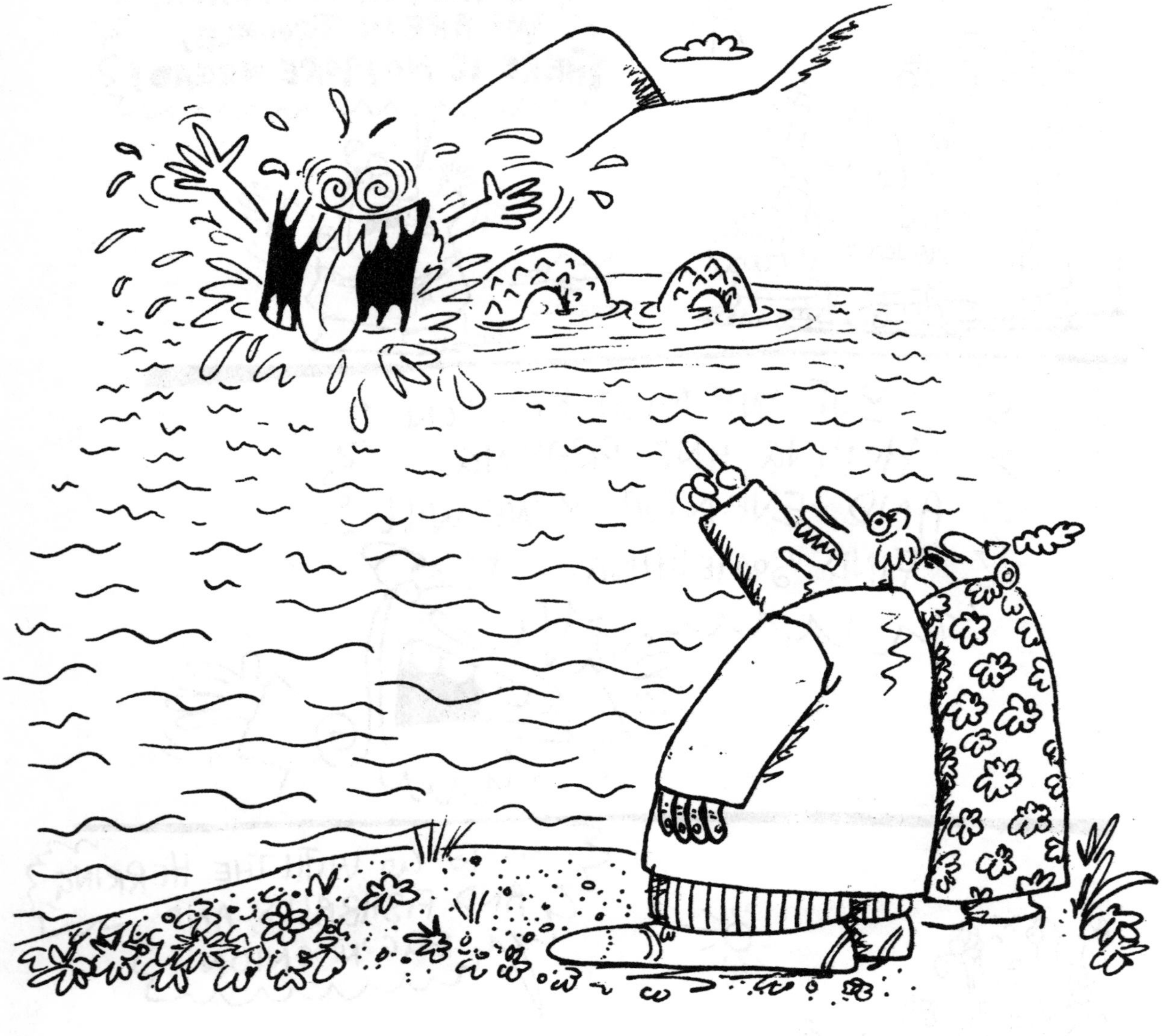

'Look honey, the Loch Ness meshuggenah!'

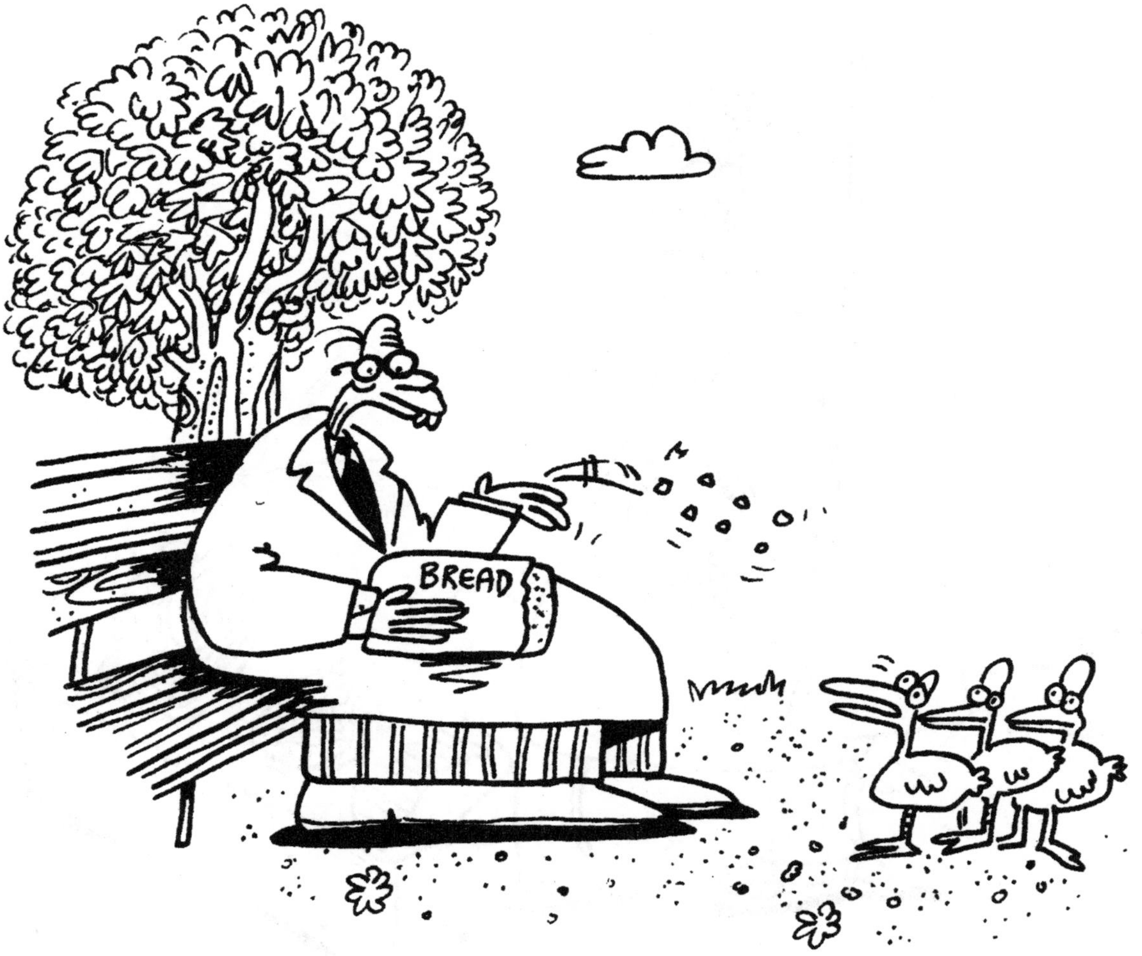
BREAD

*'Erm . . . excuse me . . . sorry to trouble you . . .
but me and the fellas were wondering . . .
Is there any chance of getting some
chopped liver to dip the bread in?'*

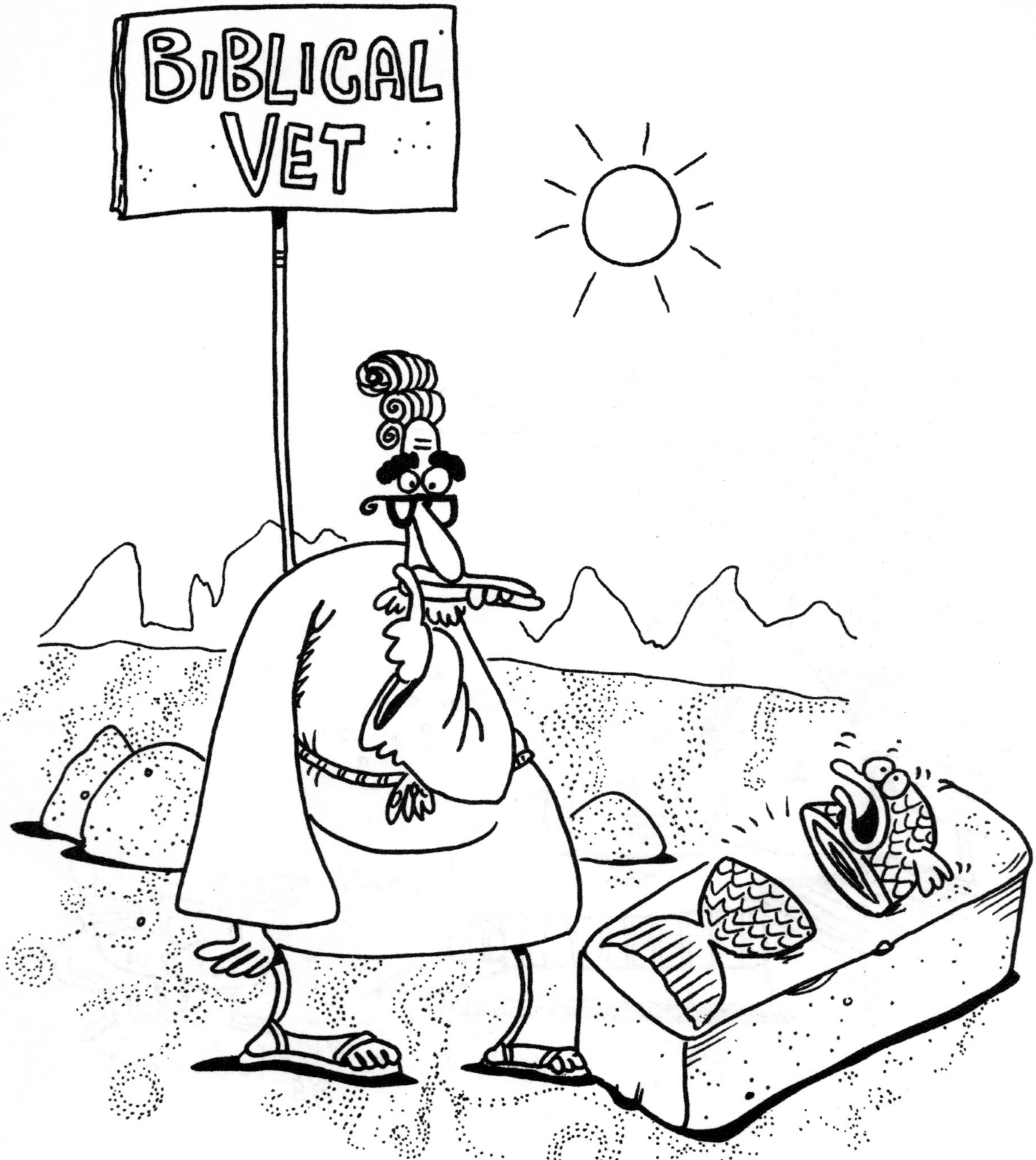
BIBLICAL VET

'One minute I'm swimming along happily in the Red Sea,
. . .the next thing I know everything starts parting!!!'

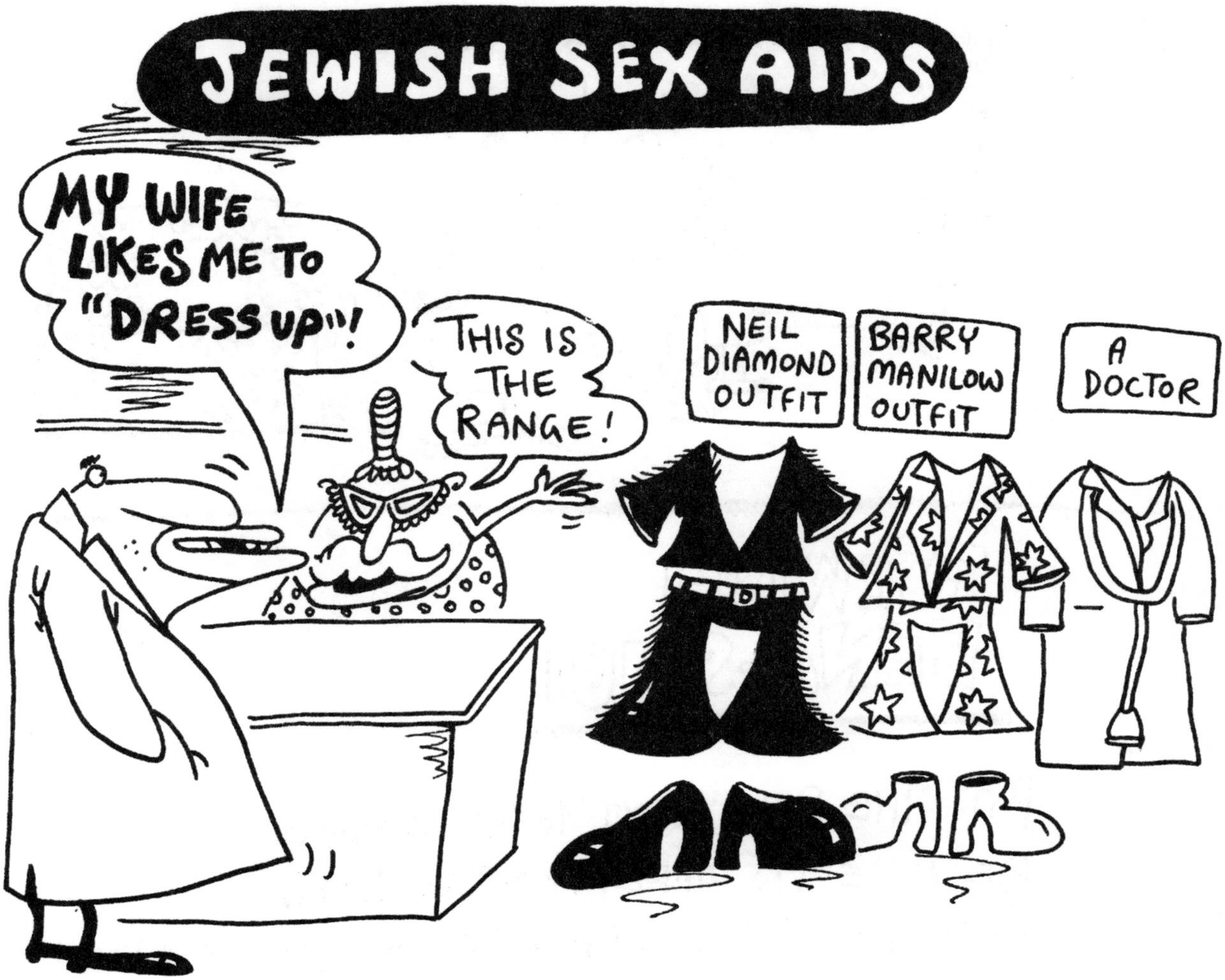

JEWISH SEX AIDS
MY WIFE LIKES ME TO "DRESS UP"!
THIS IS THE RANGE!
NEIL DIAMOND OUTFIT
BARRY MANILOW OUTFIT
A DOCTOR

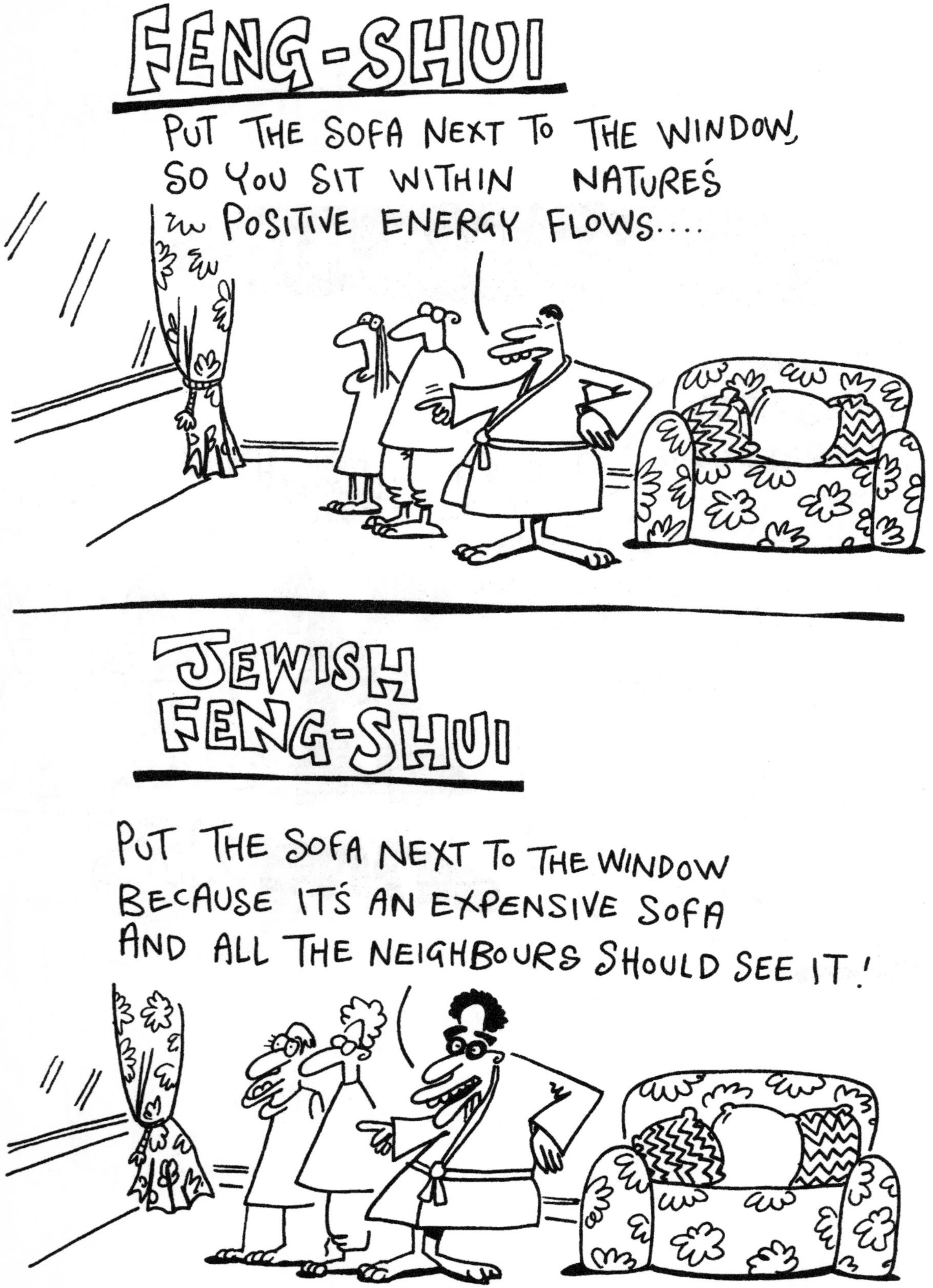
FENG-SHUI
PUT THE SOFA NEXT TO THE WINDOW, SO YOU SIT WITHIN NATURE'S POSITIVE ENERGY FLOWS....
JEWISH FENG-SHUI
PUT THE SOFA NEXT TO THE WINDOW BECAUSE IT'S AN EXPENSIVE SOFA AND ALL THE NEIGHBOURS SHOULD SEE IT!

Another Passover tale...

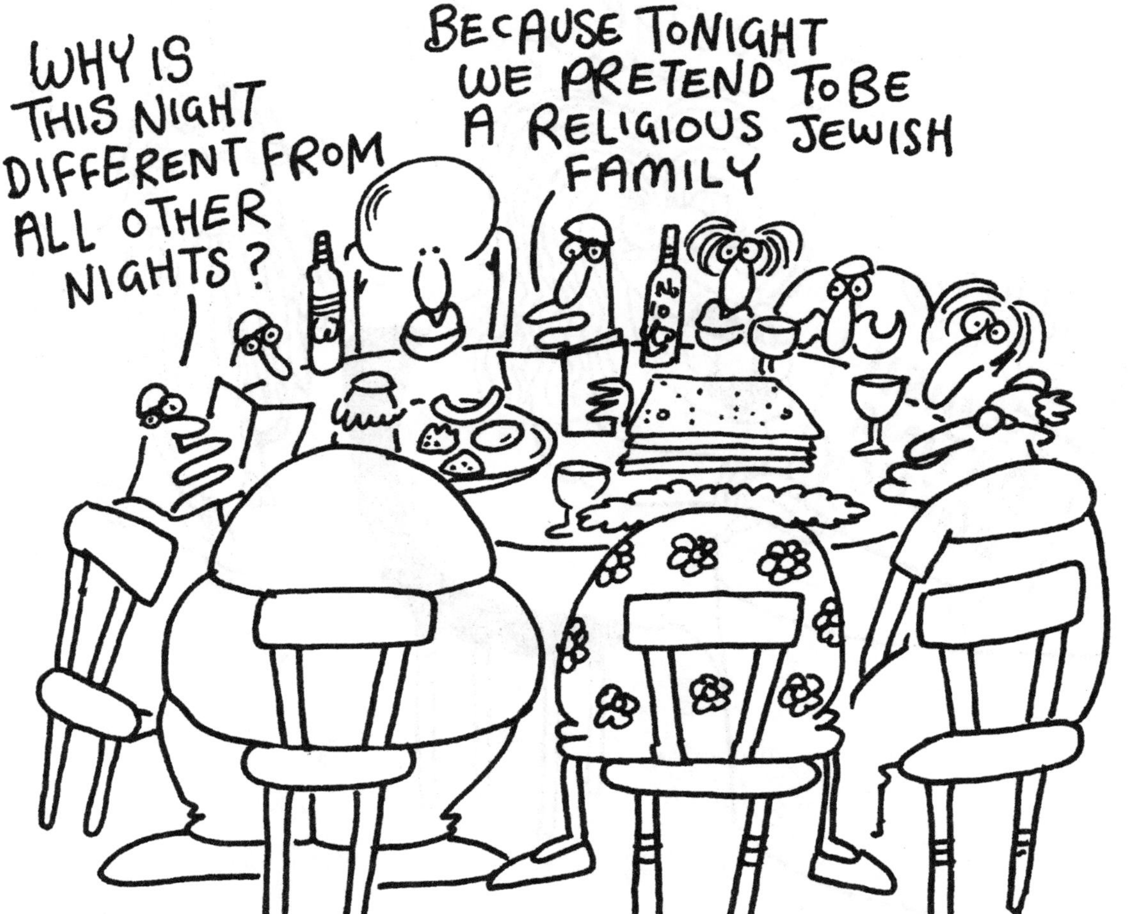
WHY IS THIS NIGHT DIFFERENT FROM ALL OTHER NIGHTS?
BECAUSE TONIGHT WE PRETEND TO BE A RELIGIOUS JEWISH FAMILY

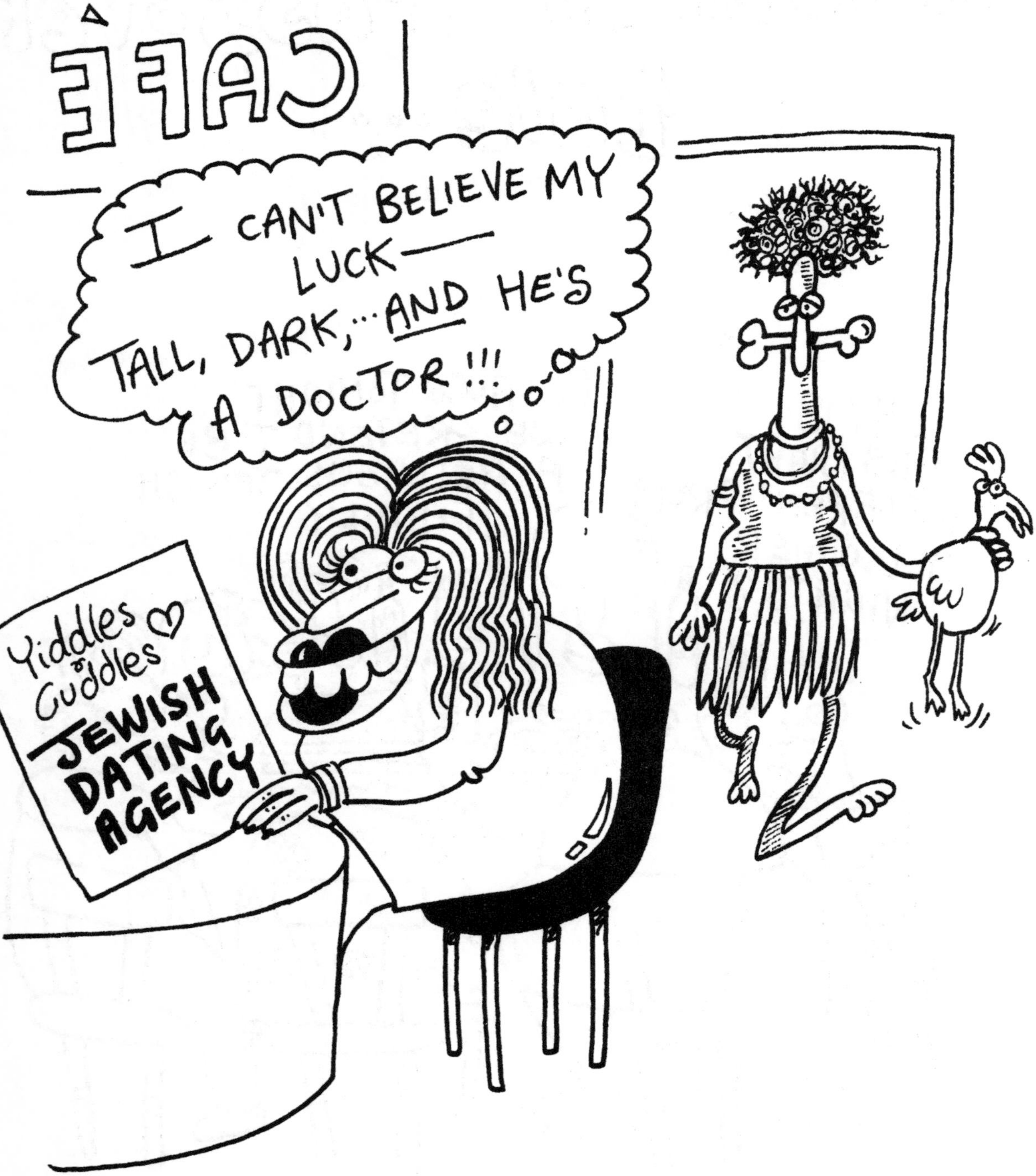
CAFÉ
I CAN'T BELIEVE MY LUCK—
TALL, DARK,... AND HE'S A DOCTOR!!!
Yiddles & Cuddles
JEWISH DATING AGENCY

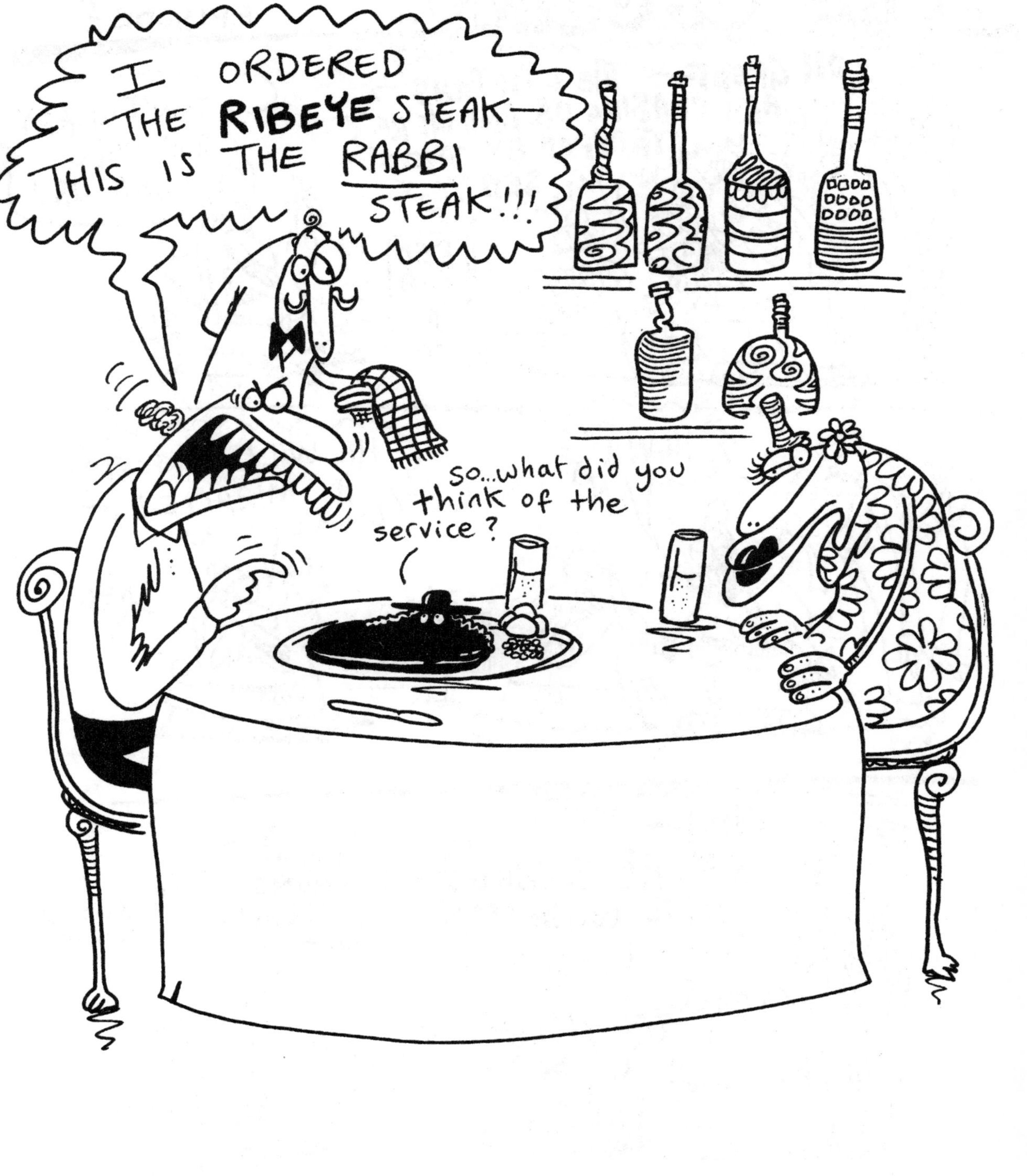
I ORDERED THE RIBEYE STEAK— THIS IS THE RABBI STEAK!!!
so...what did you think of the service?

THE CHOSEN

EPISODE 5

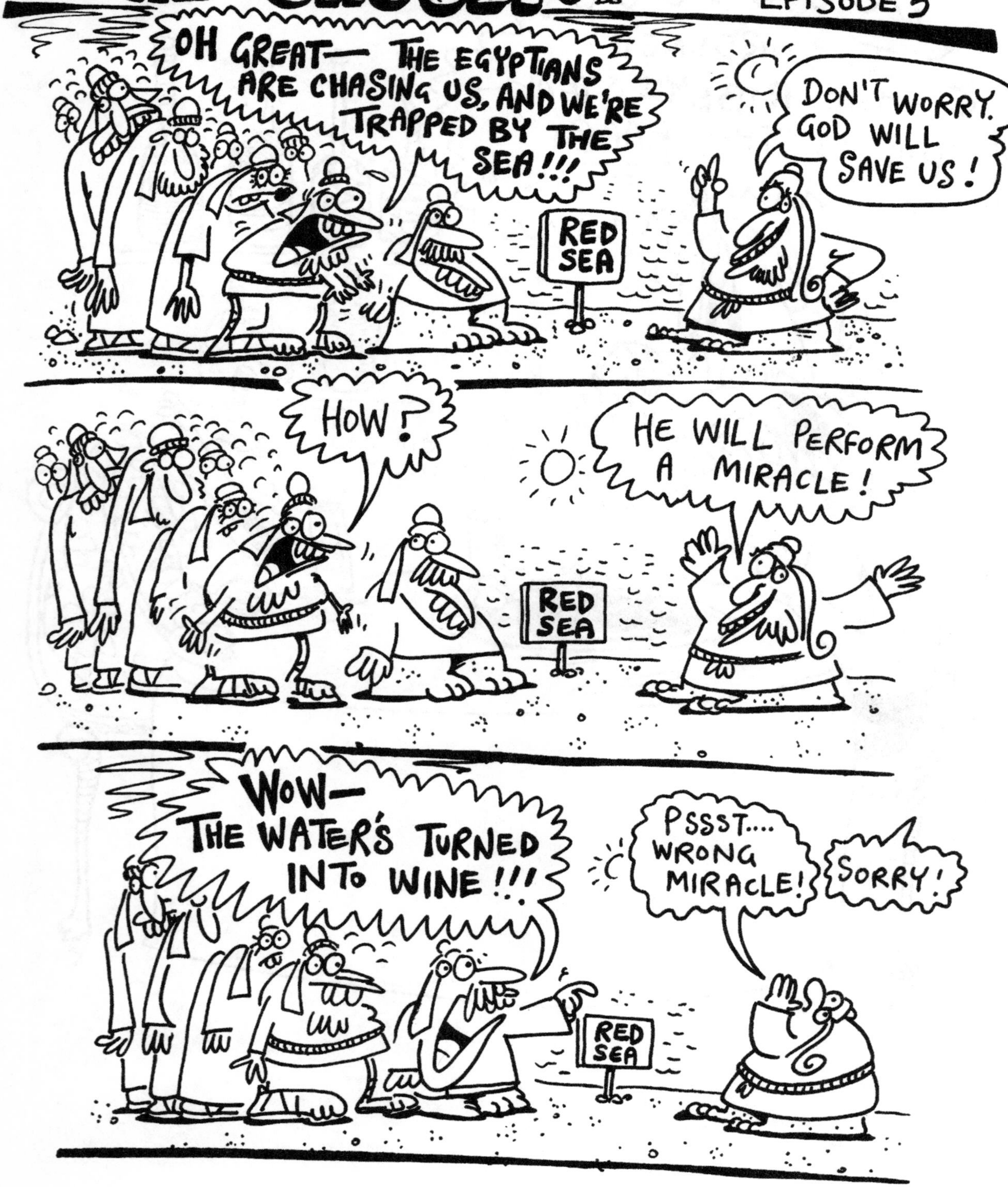
OH GREAT— THE EGYPTIANS ARE CHASING US, AND WE'RE TRAPPED BY THE SEA!!!
DON'T WORRY. GOD WILL SAVE US!
RED SEA
HOW?
HE WILL PERFORM A MIRACLE!
RED SEA
WOW— THE WATER'S TURNED INTO WINE!!!
PSSST.... WRONG MIRACLE!
SORRY!
RED SEA

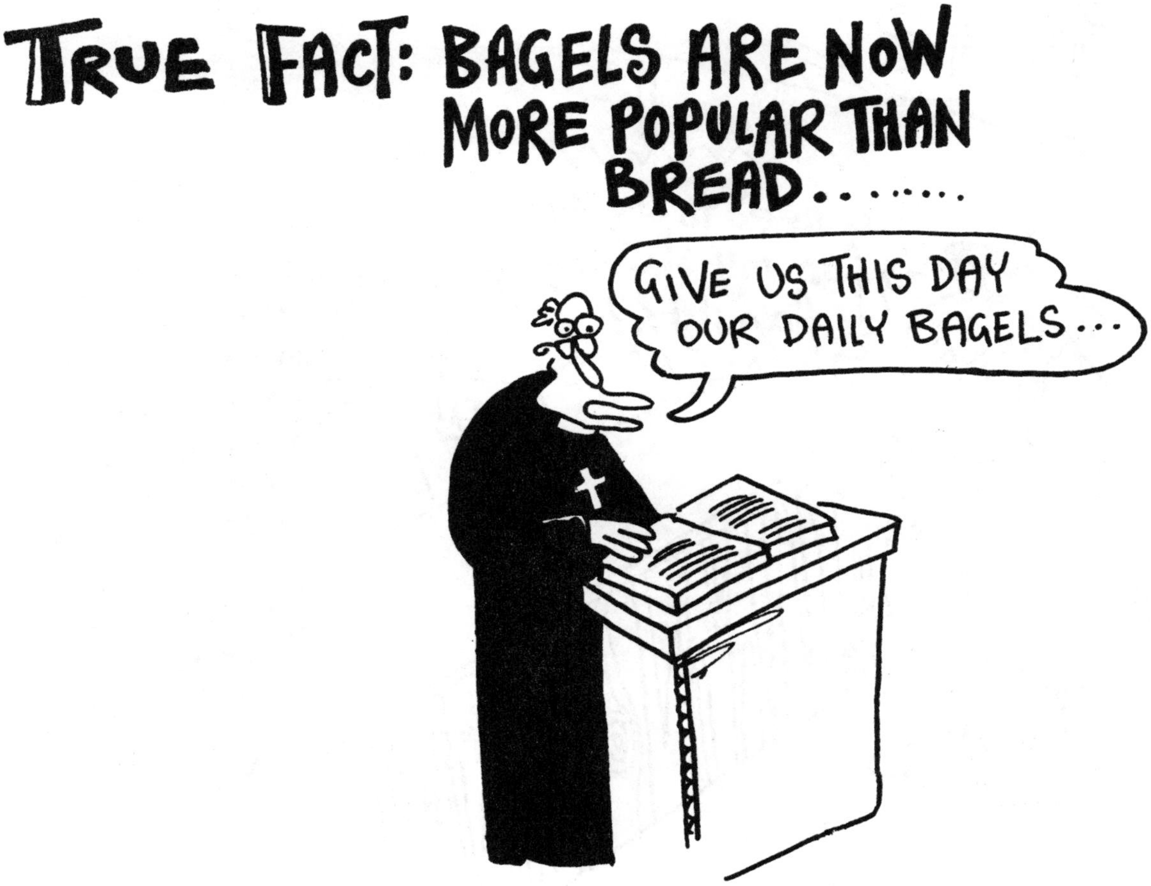
TRUE FACT: BAGELS ARE NOW MORE POPULAR THAN BREAD........
GIVE US THIS DAY OUR DAILY BAGELS...

When Jewish immigrants first came to Britain, over 100 years ago, one of the biggest problems they encountered was that they were <u>all</u> tailors.....

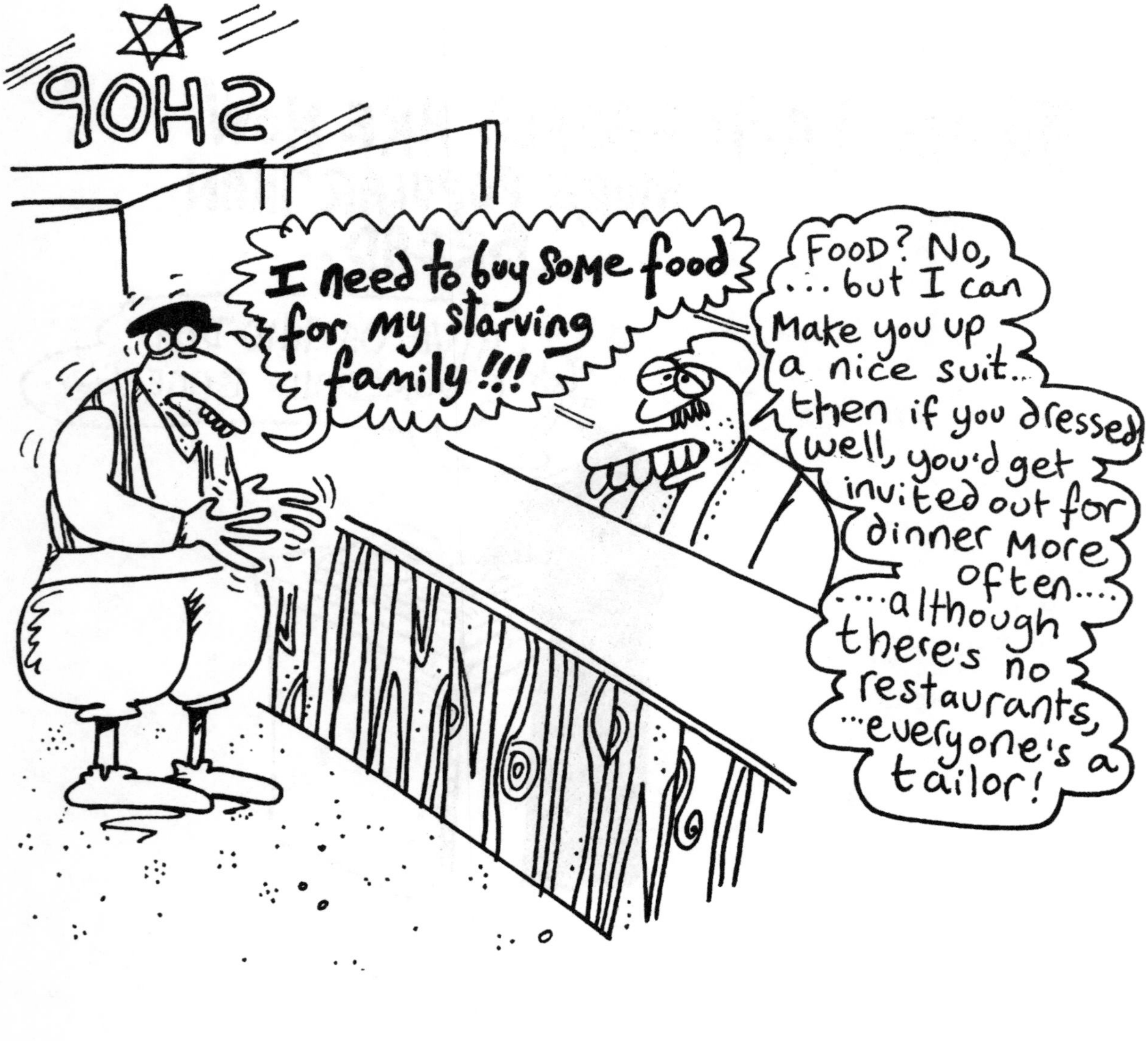
SHOP
I need to buy some food for my starving family!!!
Food? No, ... but I can make you up a nice suit... then if you dressed well, you'd get invited out for dinner more often.... ...although there's no restaurants, ...everyone's a tailor!

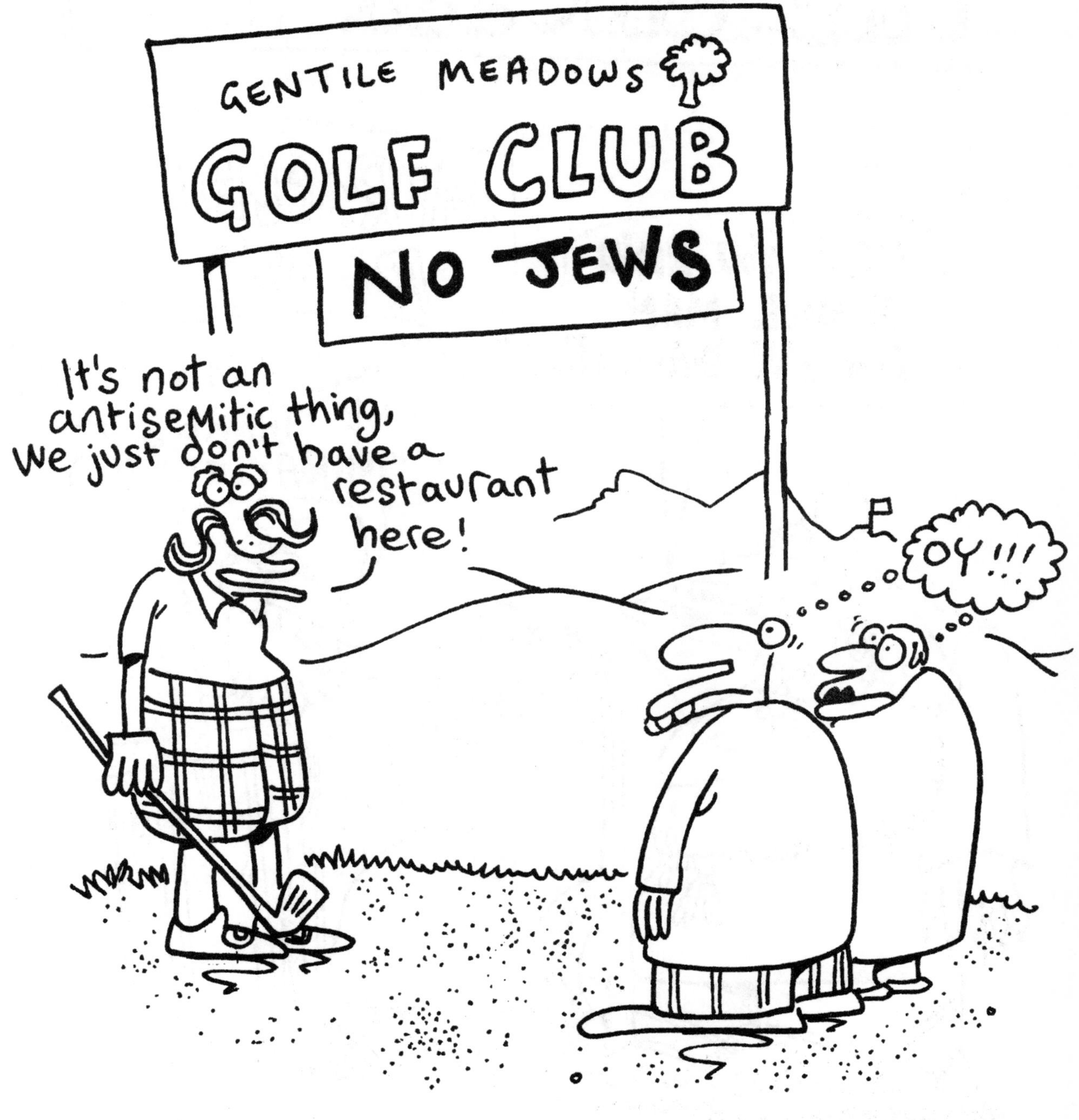
GENTILE MEADOWS
GOLF CLUB
NO JEWS
It's not an antisemitic thing, we just don't have a restaurant here!
OY!!!

THE CHOSEN EPISODE 6

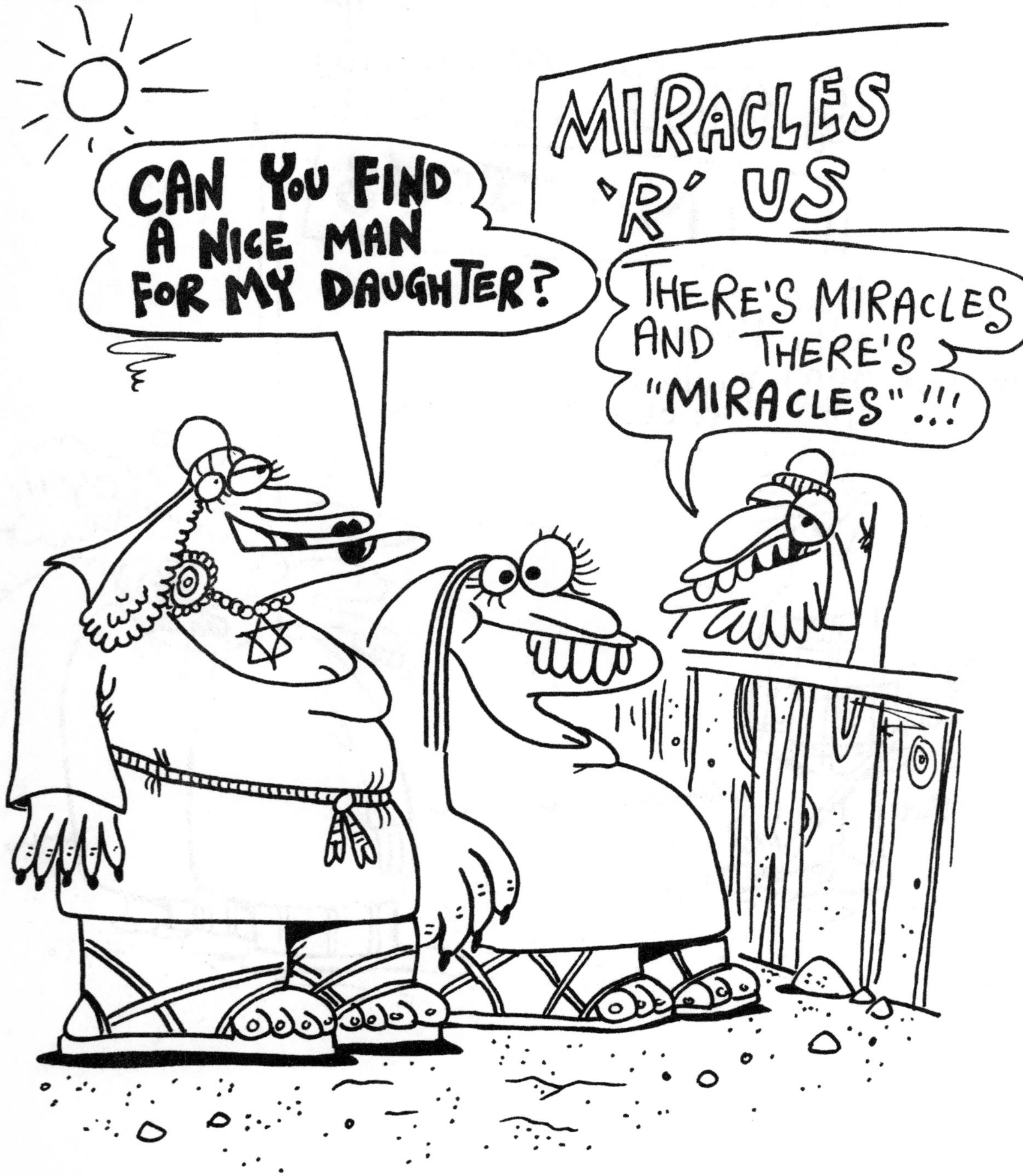
MIRACLES 'R' US
CAN YOU FIND A NICE MAN FOR MY DAUGHTER?
THERE'S MIRACLES AND THERE'S "MIRACLES"!!!

Christmas with

THE 3 WISEMANS:

OY—
WHAT A SHLAP!
AND DUSTY. IT'S SO DUSTY OUT HERE!
DID WE EAT YET?

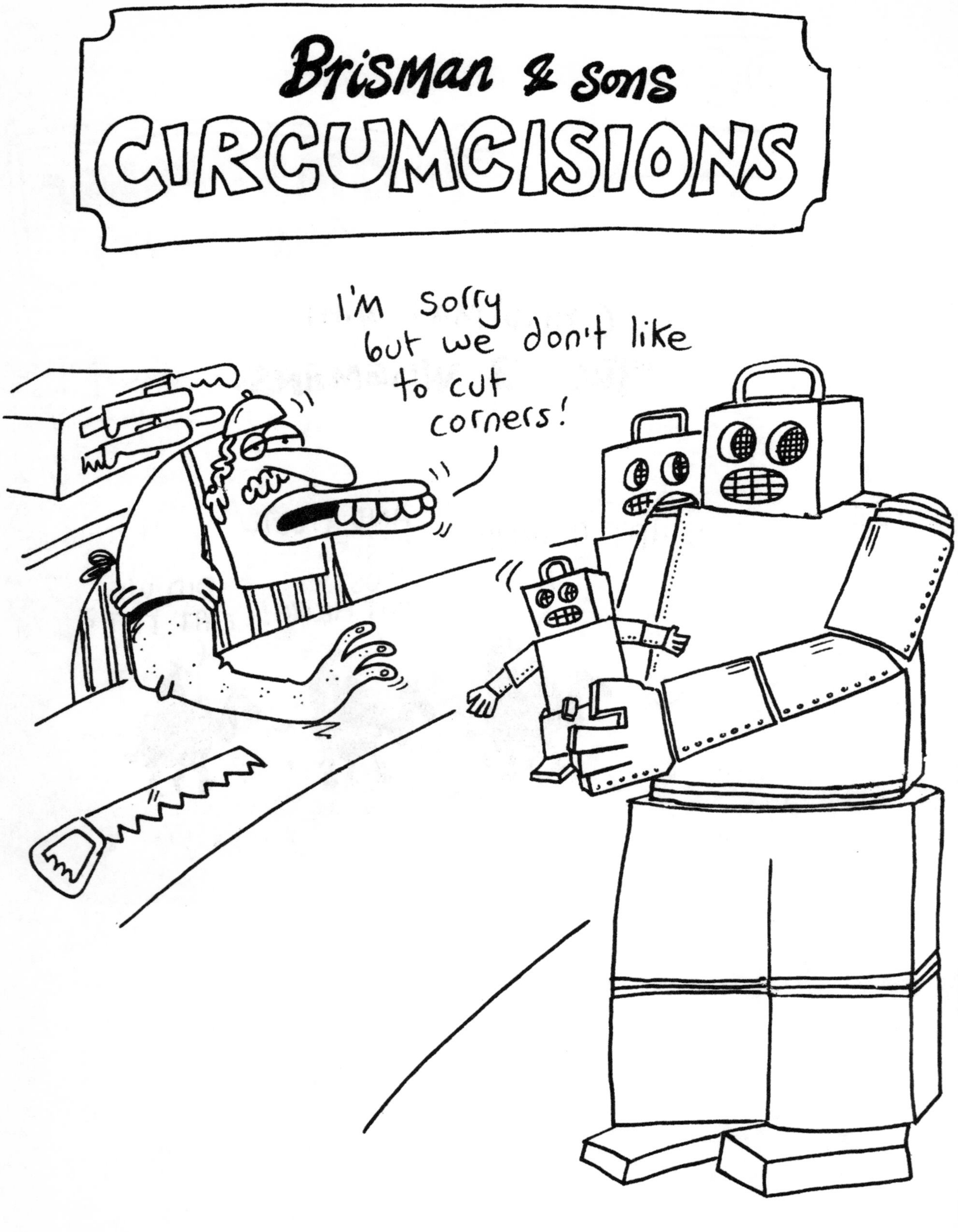
Brisman & sons
CIRCUMCISIONS
I'M sorry but we don't like to cut corners!

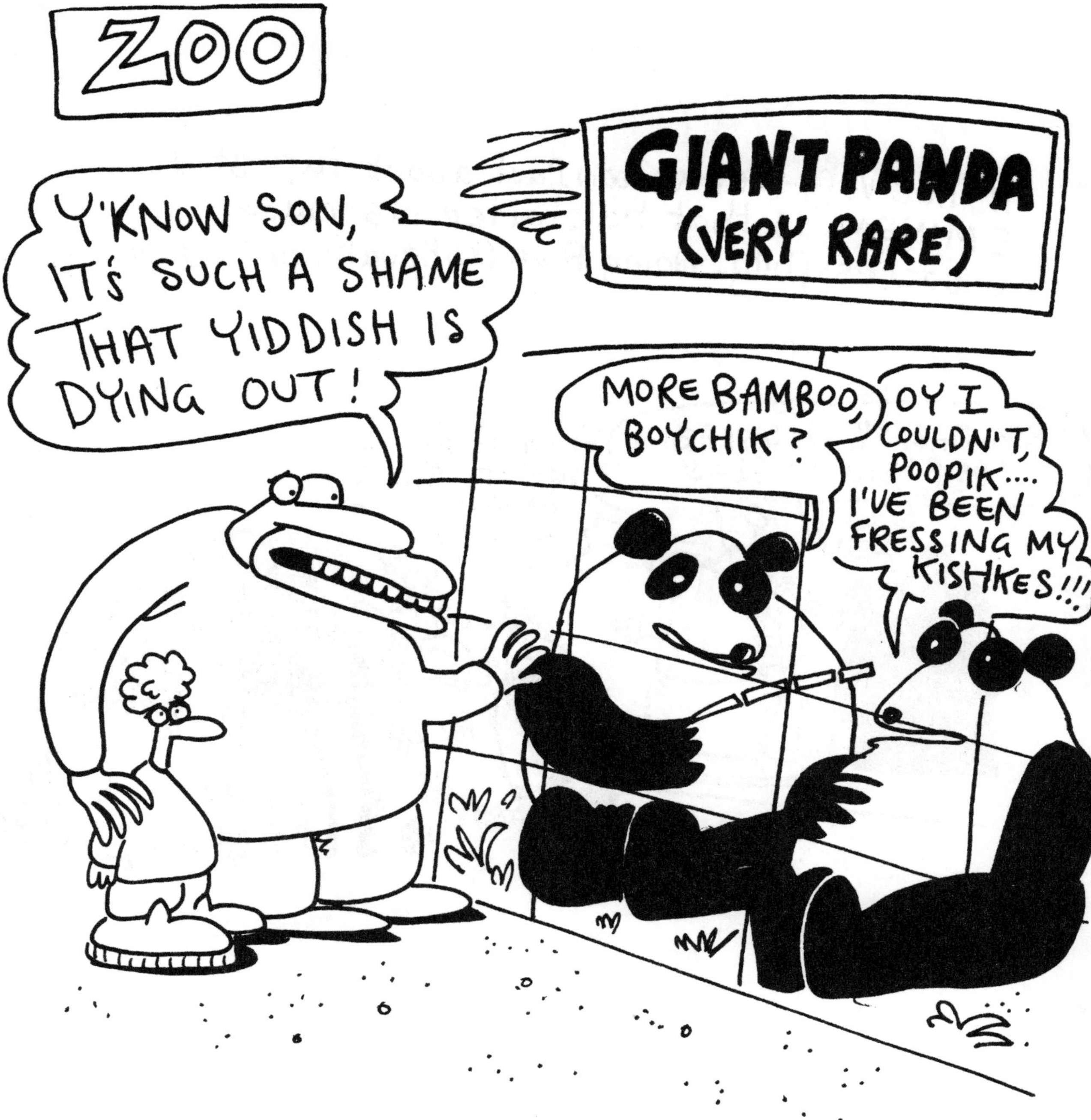
ZOO
GIANT PANDA (VERY RARE)
Y'KNOW SON, IT'S SUCH A SHAME THAT YIDDISH IS DYING OUT!
MORE BAMBOO, BOYCHIK?
OY I COULDN'T, POOPIK.... I'VE BEEN FRESSING MY KISHKES!!!

A not-very-well-known fact about rap star EMINEM is that he started his career unsuccessfully, doing Bar-Mitzvahs and weddings...

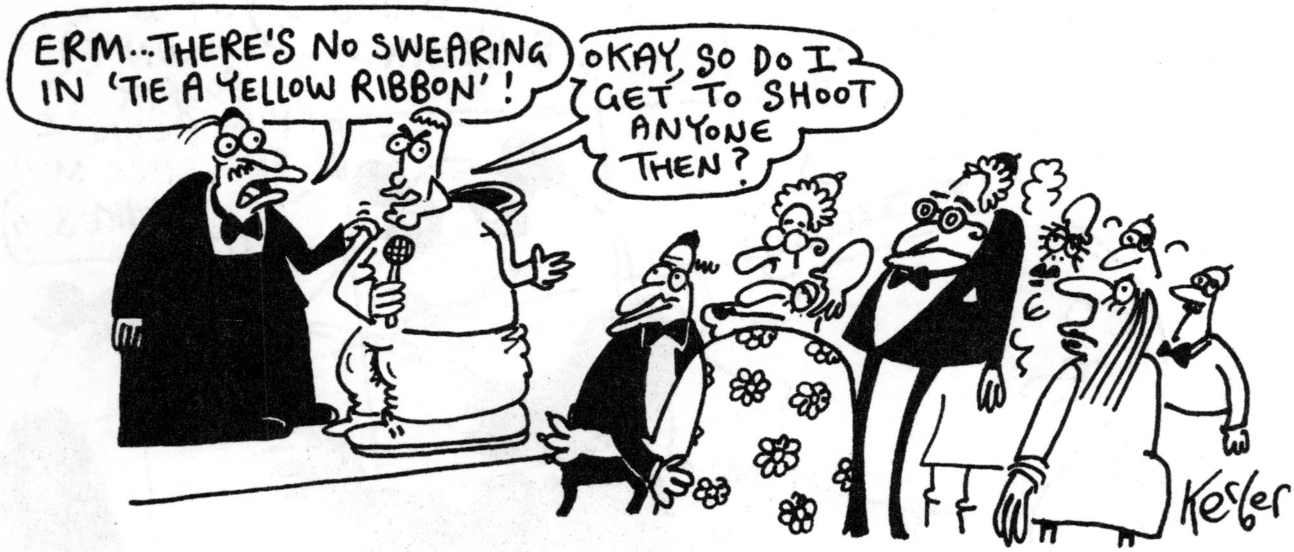

ERM...THERE'S NO SWEARING IN 'TIE A YELLOW RIBBON'!
OKAY, SO DO I GET TO SHOOT ANYONE THEN?
Kesler

1961– *Young Jerry Springer notifies the family of his career choice....*

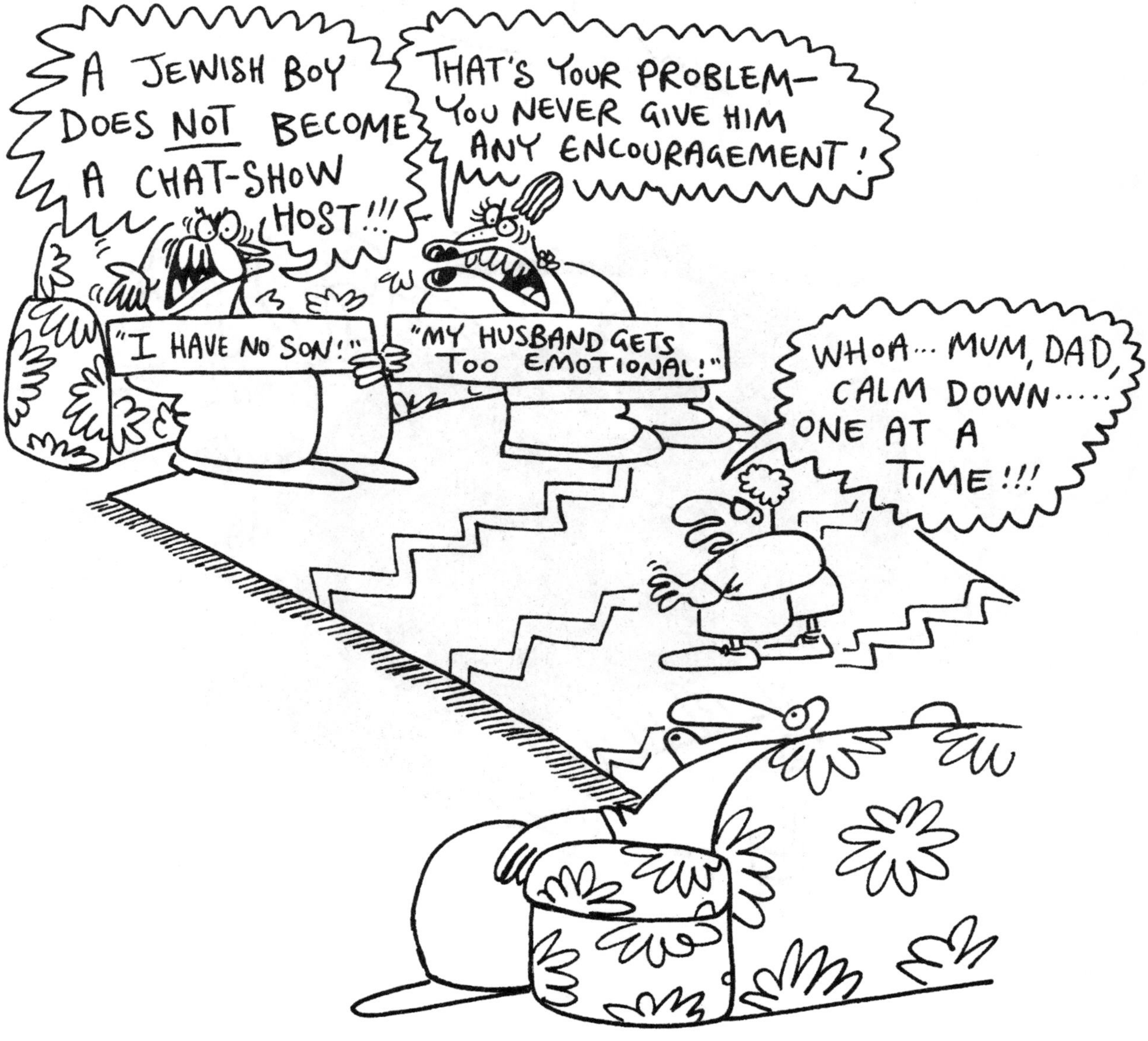
A JEWISH BOY DOES NOT BECOME A CHAT-SHOW HOST!!!
THAT'S YOUR PROBLEM– YOU NEVER GIVE HIM ANY ENCOURAGEMENT!
"I HAVE NO SON!"
"MY HUSBAND GETS TOO EMOTIONAL!"
WHOA... MUM, DAD, CALM DOWN..... ONE AT A TIME!!!

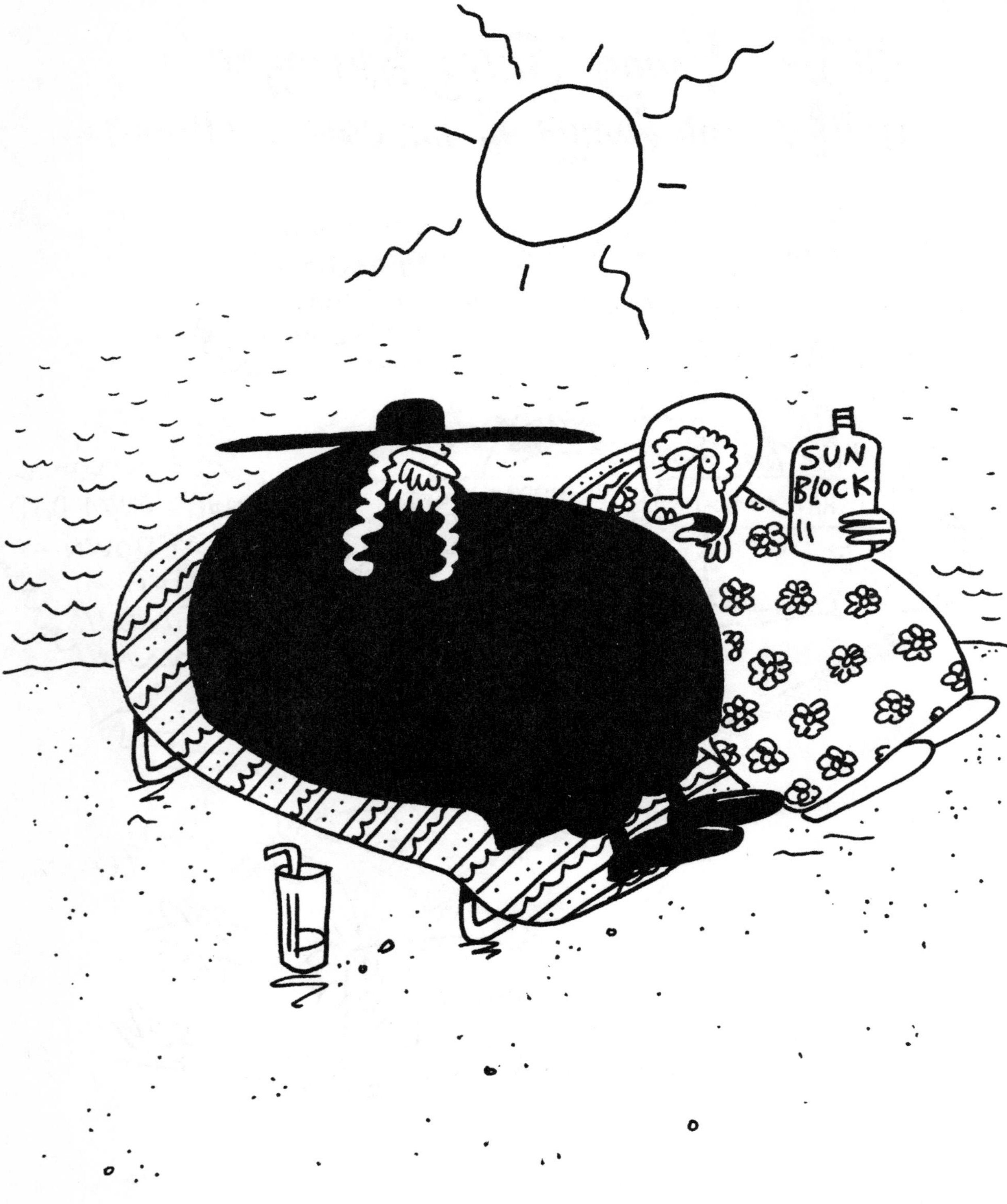
SUN
BLOCK

'Put some of this on, you'll burn!'

A Jewish poker game hots up....

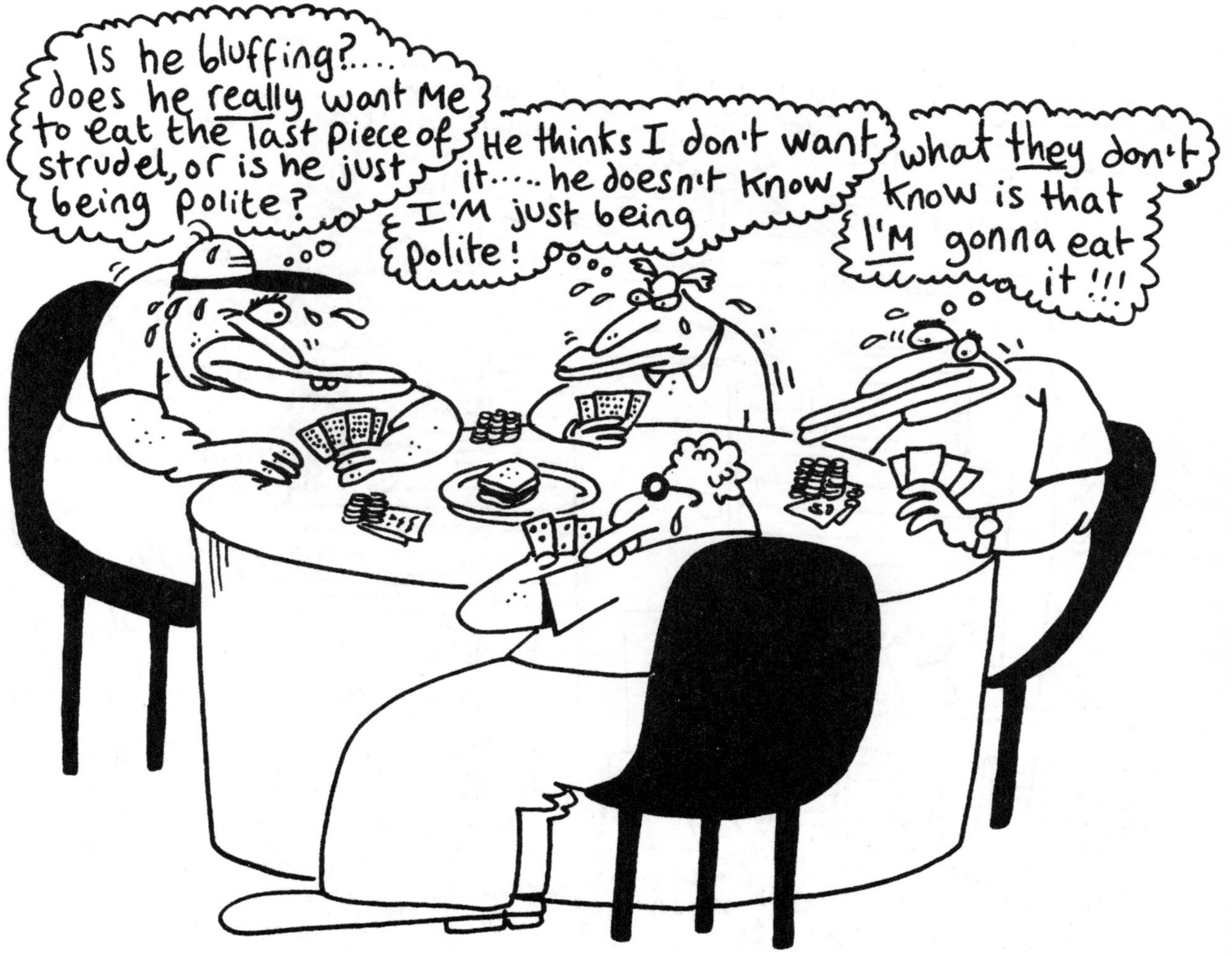
Is he bluffing?.... does he really want me to eat the last piece of strudel, or is he just being polite?
He thinks I don't want it.... he doesn't know I'M just being polite!
what they don't know is that I'M gonna eat it!!!

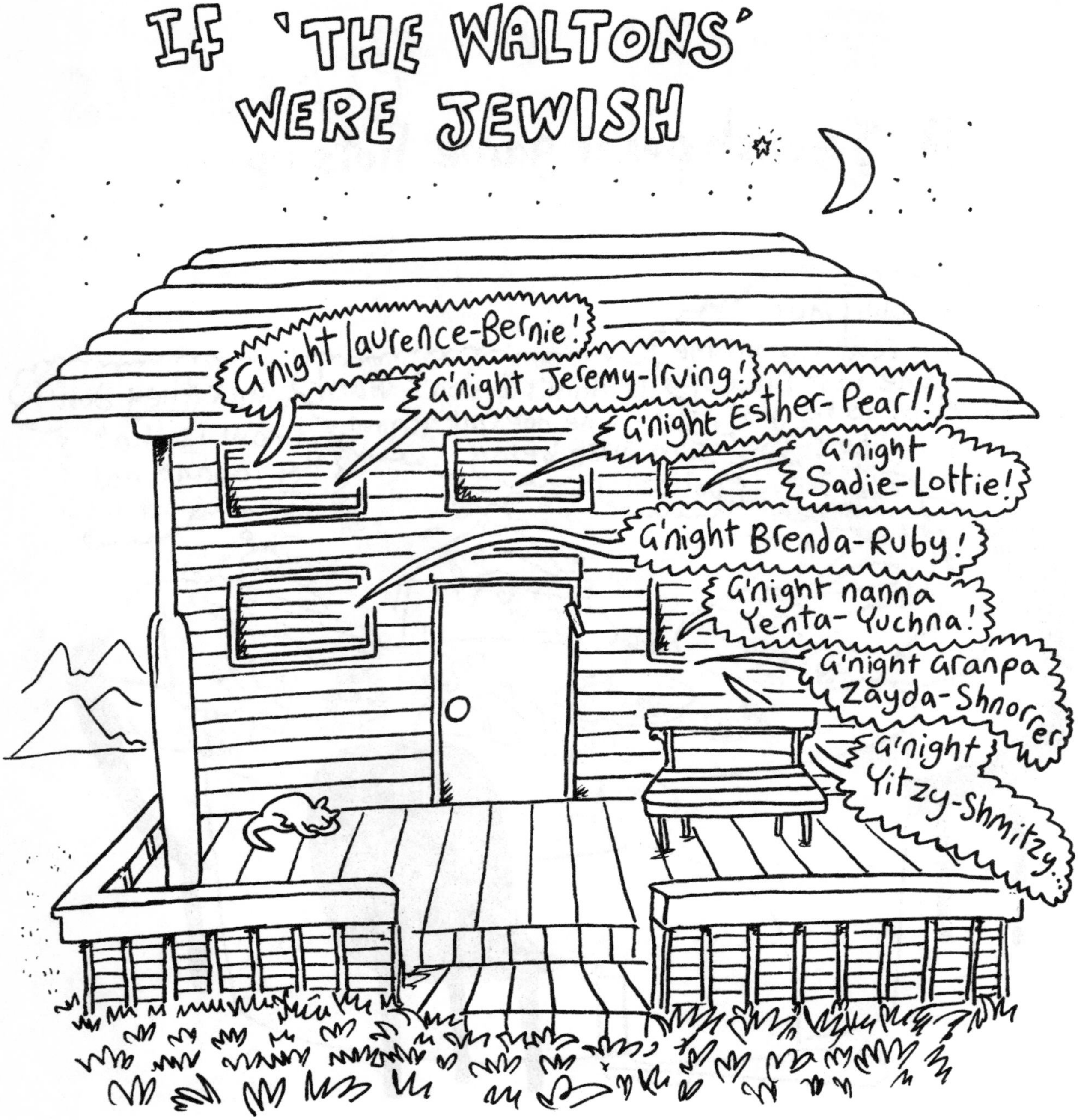

IF 'THE WALTONS' WERE JEWISH
G'night Laurence-Bernie!
G'night Jeremy-Irving!
G'night Esther-Pearl!
G'night Sadie-Lottie!
G'night Brenda-Ruby!
G'night nanna Yenta-Yuchna!
G'night Granpa Zayda-Shnorrer
G'night Yitzy-Shmitzy...

JEWISH SUPERMODELS

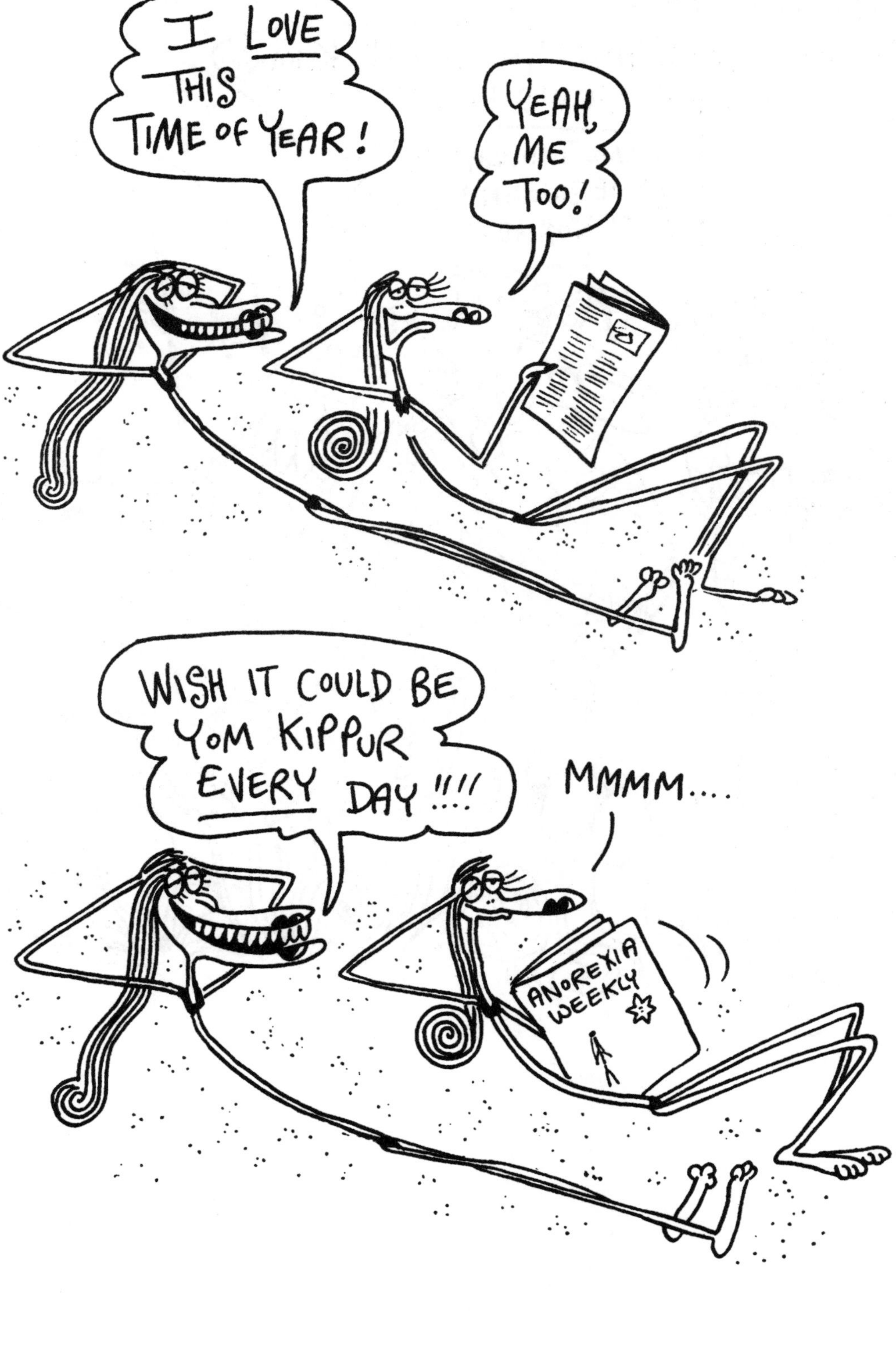
I LOVE THIS TIME OF YEAR!
YEAH, ME TOO!
WISH IT COULD BE YOM KIPPUR EVERY DAY!!!!
MMMM....
ANOREXIA WEEKLY

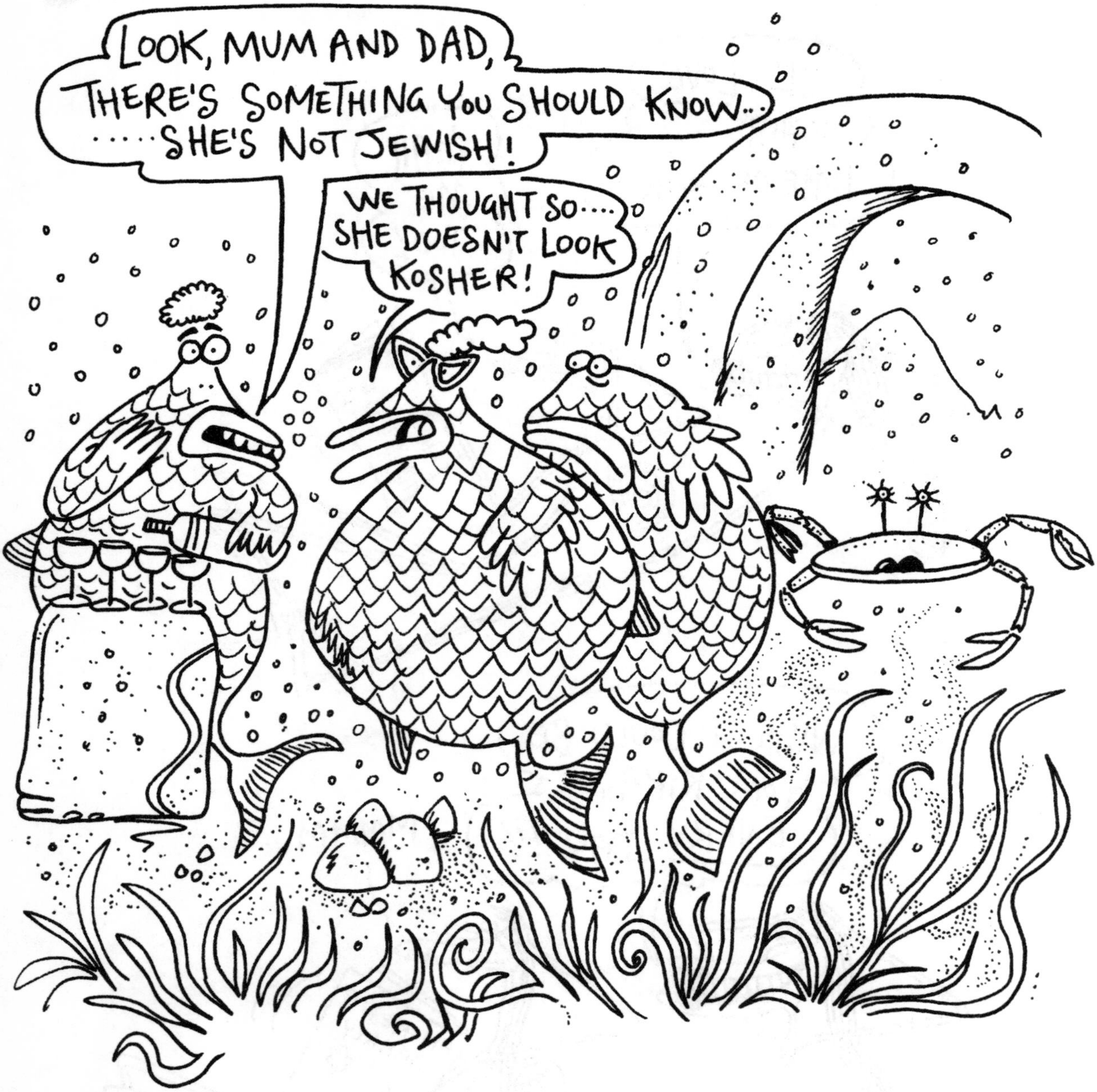
LOOK, MUM AND DAD, THERE'S SOMETHING YOU SHOULD KNOW.. .....SHE'S NOT JEWISH!
WE THOUGHT SO..... SHE DOESN'T LOOK KOSHER!

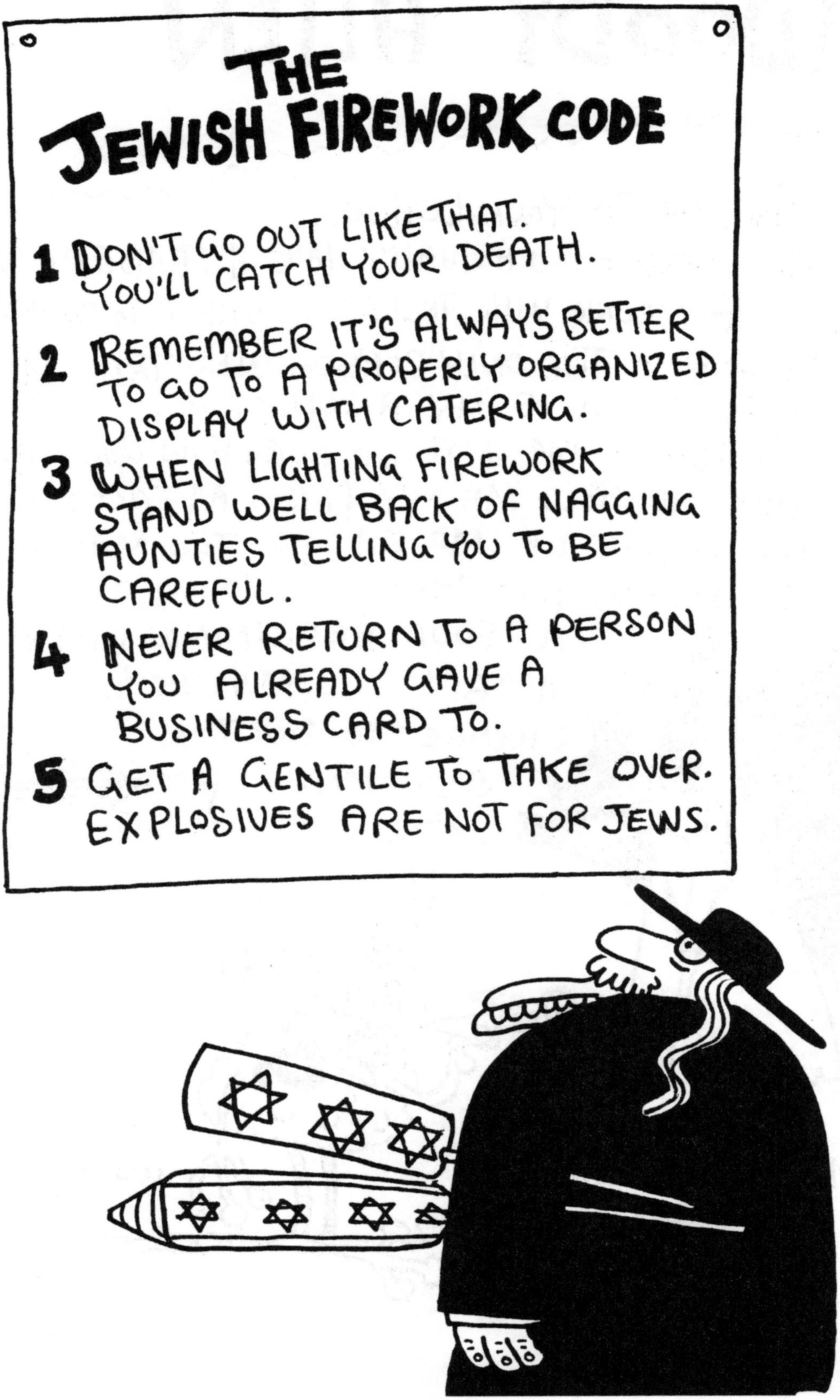
THE JEWISH FIREWORK CODE
1 DON'T GO OUT LIKE THAT. YOU'LL CATCH YOUR DEATH.
2 REMEMBER IT'S ALWAYS BETTER TO GO TO A PROPERLY ORGANIZED DISPLAY WITH CATERING.
3 WHEN LIGHTING FIREWORK STAND WELL BACK OF NAGGING AUNTIES TELLING YOU TO BE CAREFUL.
4 NEVER RETURN TO A PERSON YOU ALREADY GAVE A BUSINESS CARD TO.
5 GET A GENTILE TO TAKE OVER. EXPLOSIVES ARE NOT FOR JEWS.

WOODY ALIEN

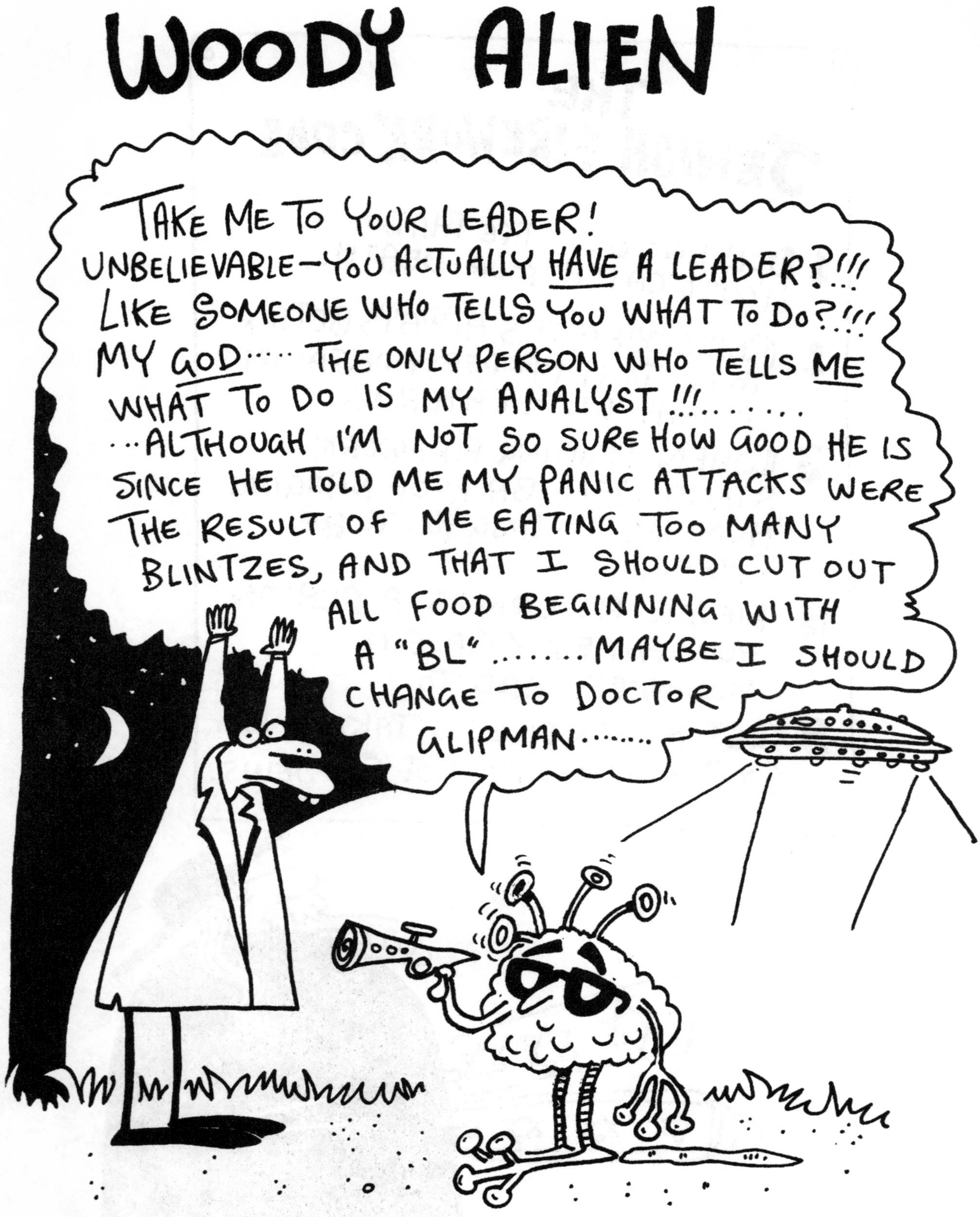
TAKE ME TO YOUR LEADER! UNBELIEVABLE—YOU ACTUALLY HAVE A LEADER?!!! LIKE SOMEONE WHO TELLS YOU WHAT TO DO?!!! MY GOD..... THE ONLY PERSON WHO TELLS ME WHAT TO DO IS MY ANALYST!!!........ ...ALTHOUGH I'M NOT SO SURE HOW GOOD HE IS SINCE HE TOLD ME MY PANIC ATTACKS WERE THE RESULT OF ME EATING TOO MANY BLINTZES, AND THAT I SHOULD CUT OUT ALL FOOD BEGINNING WITH A "BL"....... MAYBE I SHOULD CHANGE TO DOCTOR GLIPMAN........

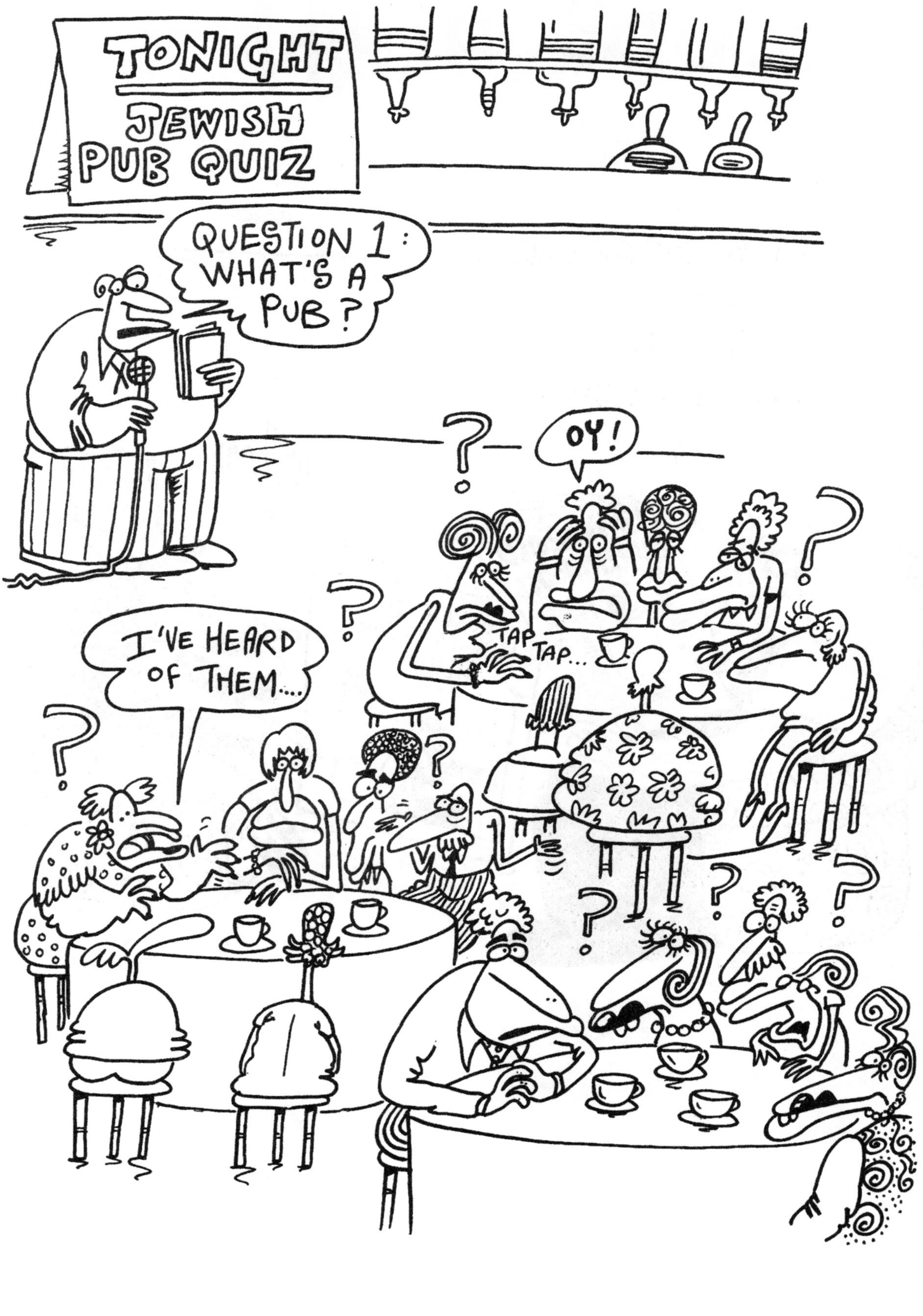
TONIGHT
JEWISH PUB QUIZ
QUESTION 1: WHAT'S A PUB?
OY!
TAP TAP...
I'VE HEARD OF THEM....

IT'S DISGUSTING-
A KID
POSING
LIKE AN ADULT!!!
13 YEAR OLD
SUPERMODEL
JEREMY'S
BAR-MITZVAH
ALBUM

ADVERTISEMENT

PRESENTING

"Little Jewish Auntie"

A fine collector plate edged with 22 carat gold

A collector's treasure- a perfect gift

"Little Jewish Auntie" will be a beautiful addition to your home. It can be yours for just £3,985.00 (plus p+p)

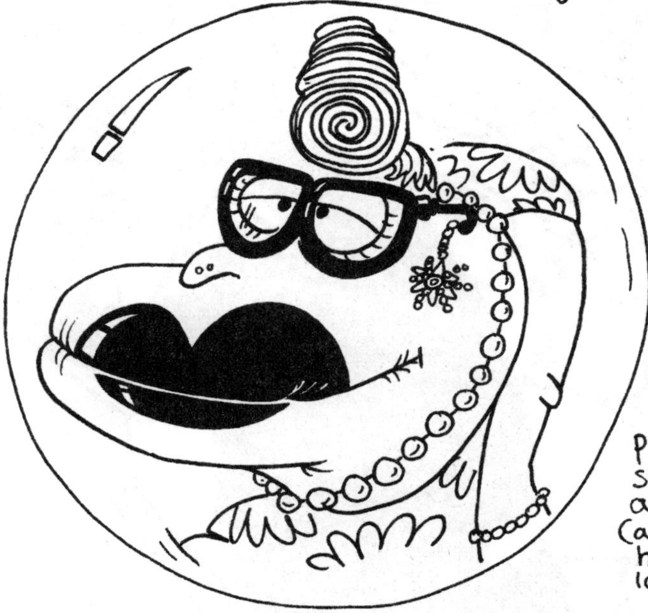

Plate shown slightly bigger than actual size (although it depends how closely you're looking at this page)

"I was delighted when my neighbour invited me to meet his little auntie," says artist Sheldon Moygul.....

"What an adorable little auntie, so lovely and affectionate, and her face held a hint of mischief.....I just knew I would have to paint her!"

☐ Please charge my credit/debit card.

☐ Mastercard ☐ Visa/Delta

Card No: ☐☐☐☐☐☐☐☐☐☐☐☐☐☐☐☐

Card expiry date:______________

Signature:__________________________

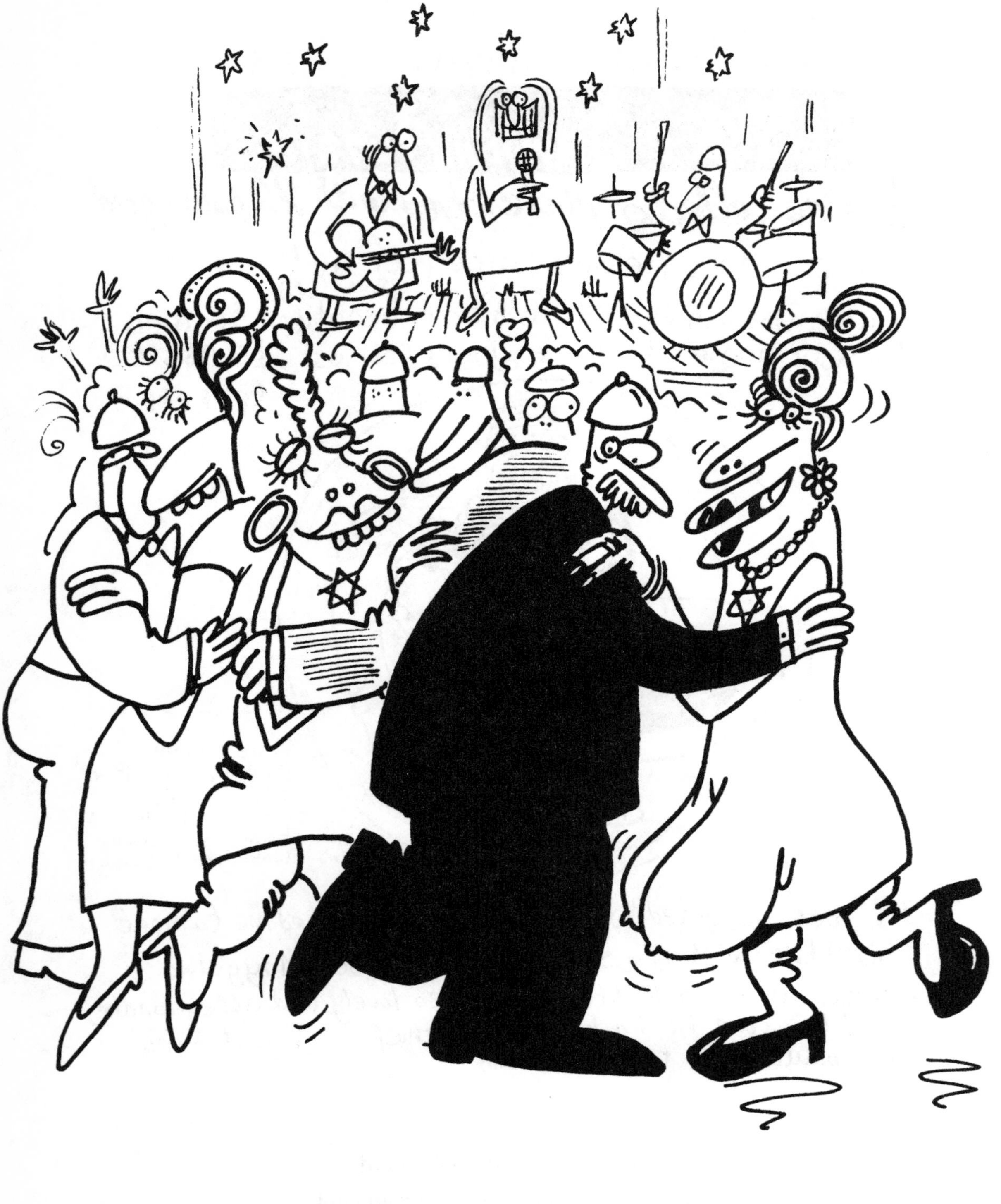

*"I had the silicone implants done in '98 . . .
. . . the year before I took up trampolinig!"*

GOLDZILLA

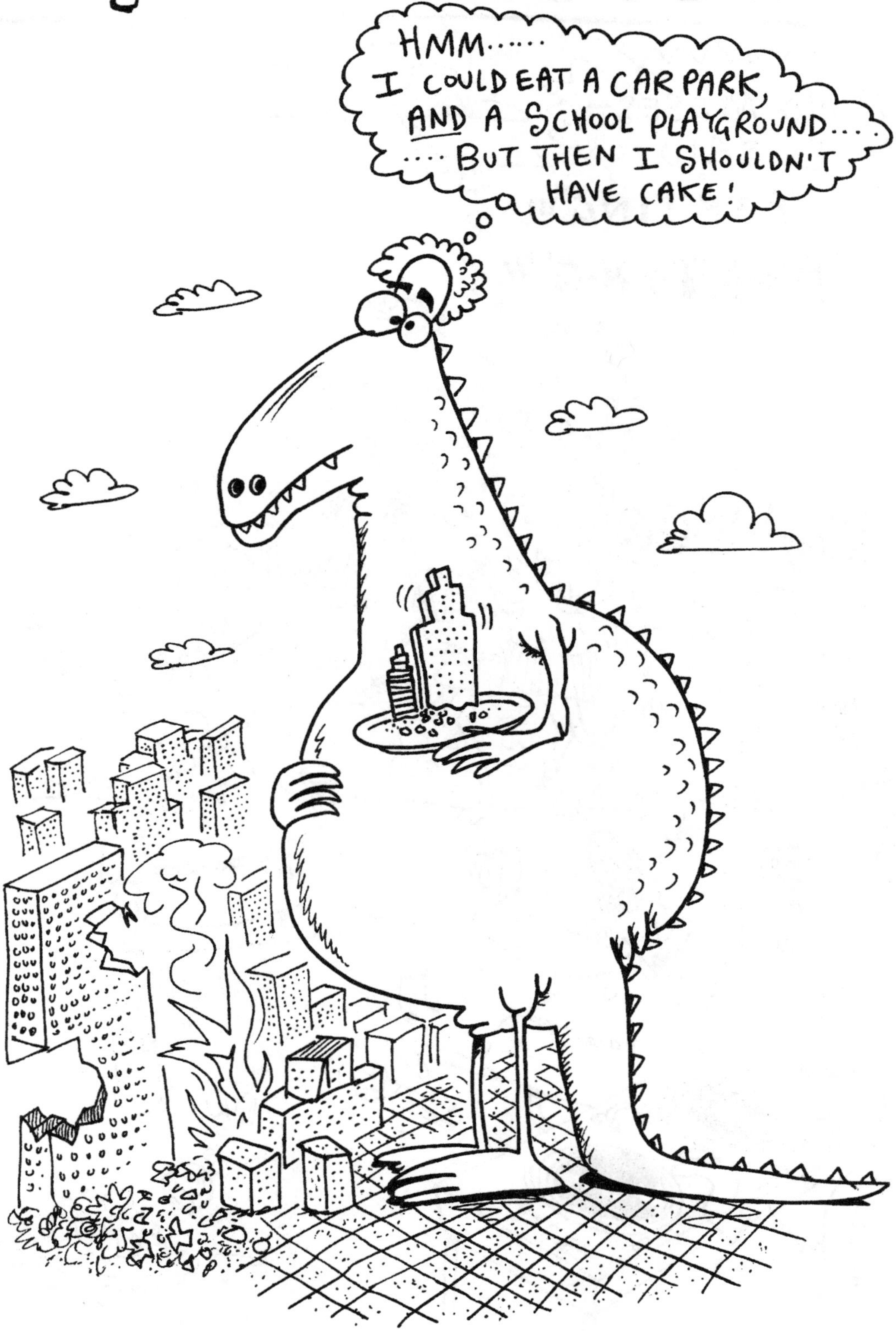
HMM......
I COULD EAT A CAR PARK,
AND A SCHOOL PLAYGROUND....
.... BUT THEN I SHOULDN'T
HAVE CAKE!

THE CHOSEN EPISODE 7

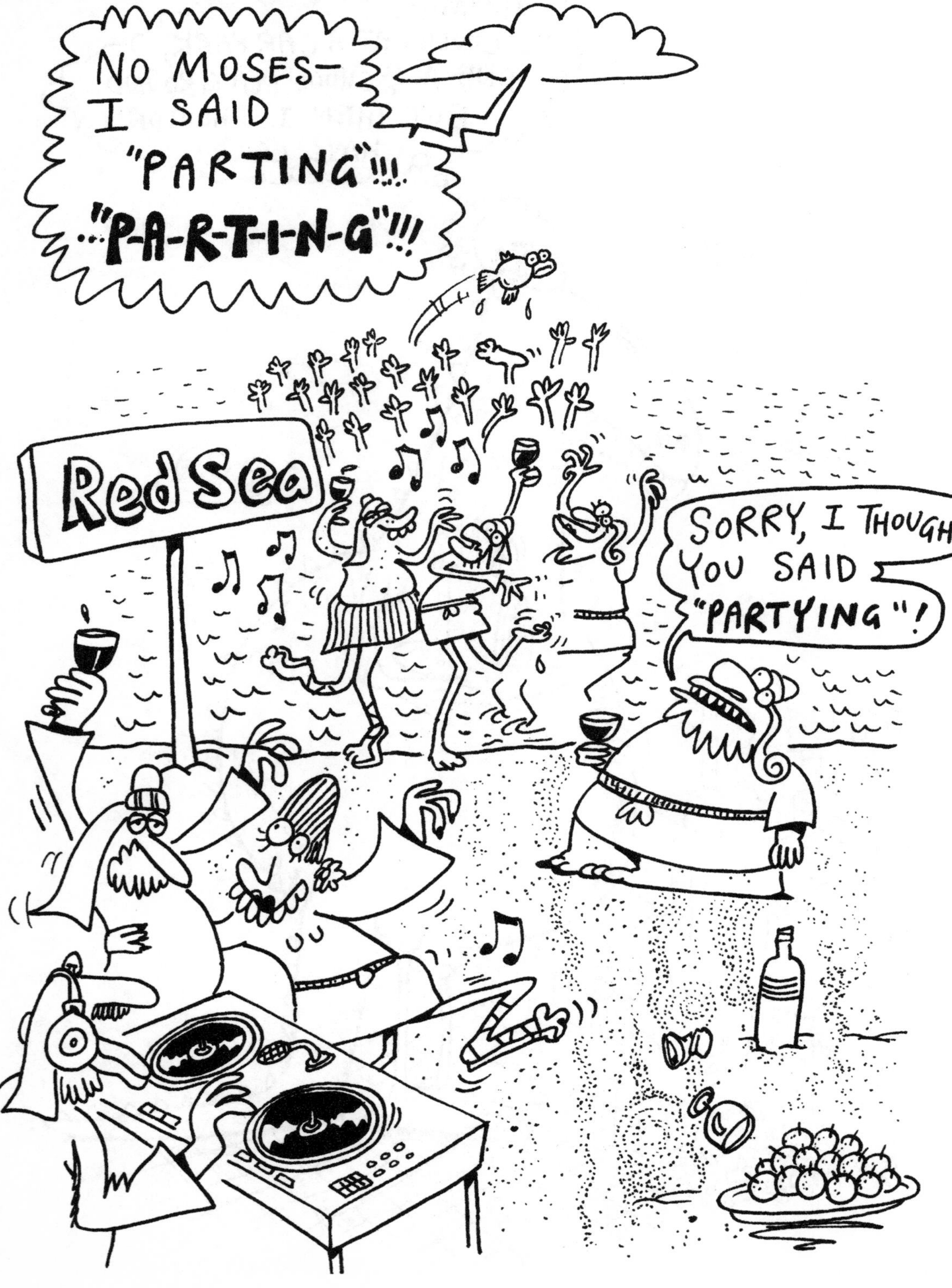

NO MOSES- I SAID "PARTING"!!!.. .."P-A-R-T-I-N-G"!!!
Red Sea
SORRY, I THOUGHT YOU SAID "PARTYING"!

The Headless Horseman goes to Synagogue......

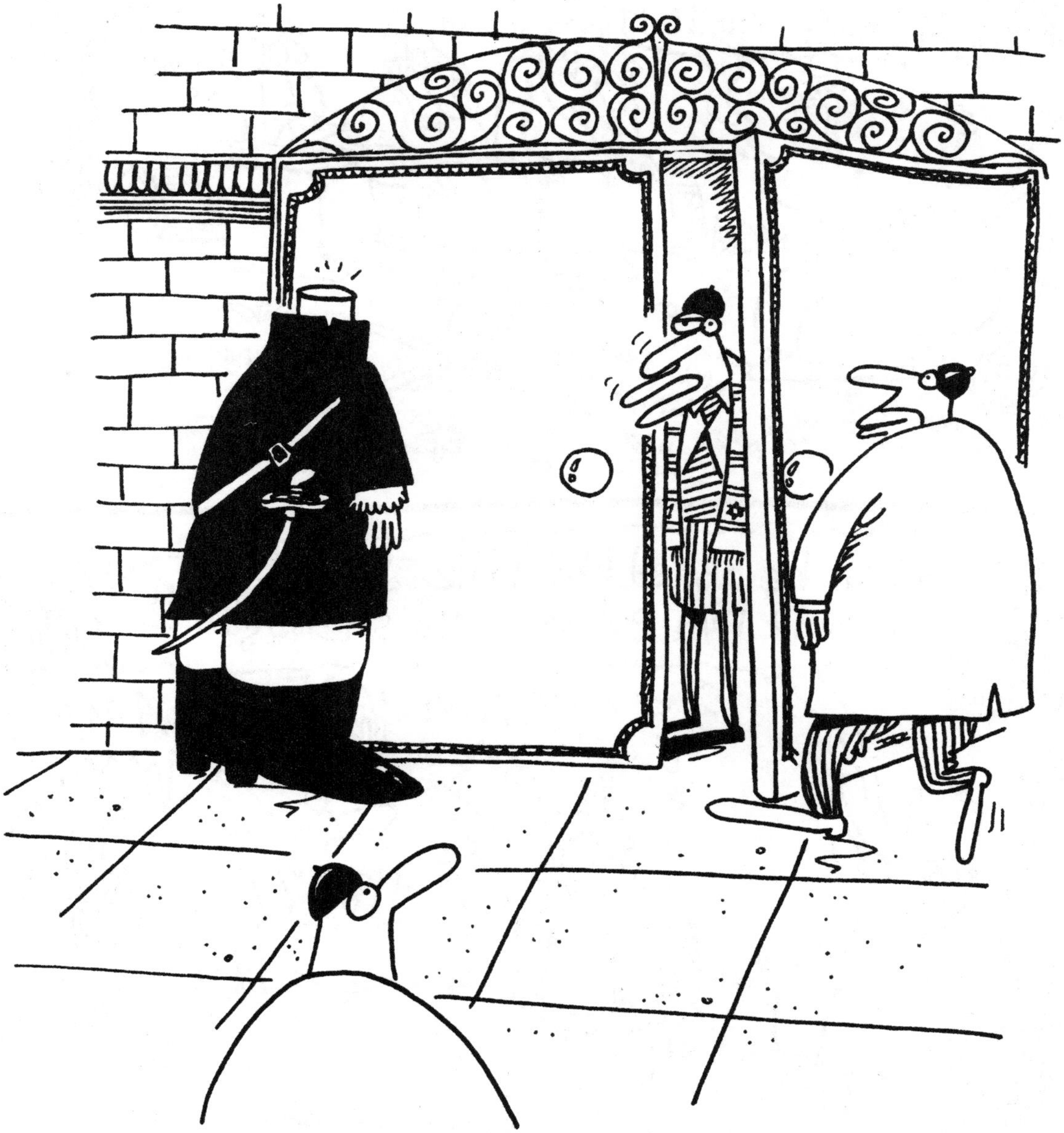

"Excuse me, would you mind covering your neck?"

JEWISH CAMPFIRE STORIES:

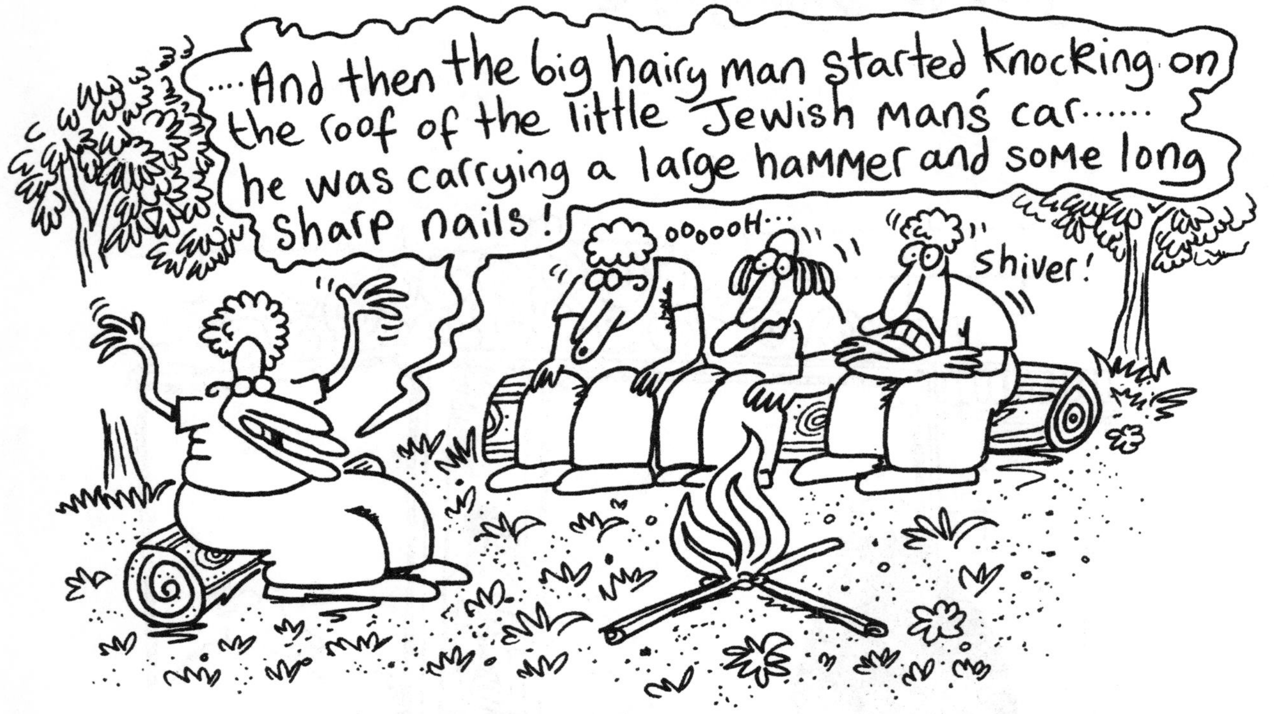

....And then the big hairy man started knocking on the roof of the little Jewish man's car...... he was carrying a large hammer and some long sharp nails!
OOOOOH...
Shiver!

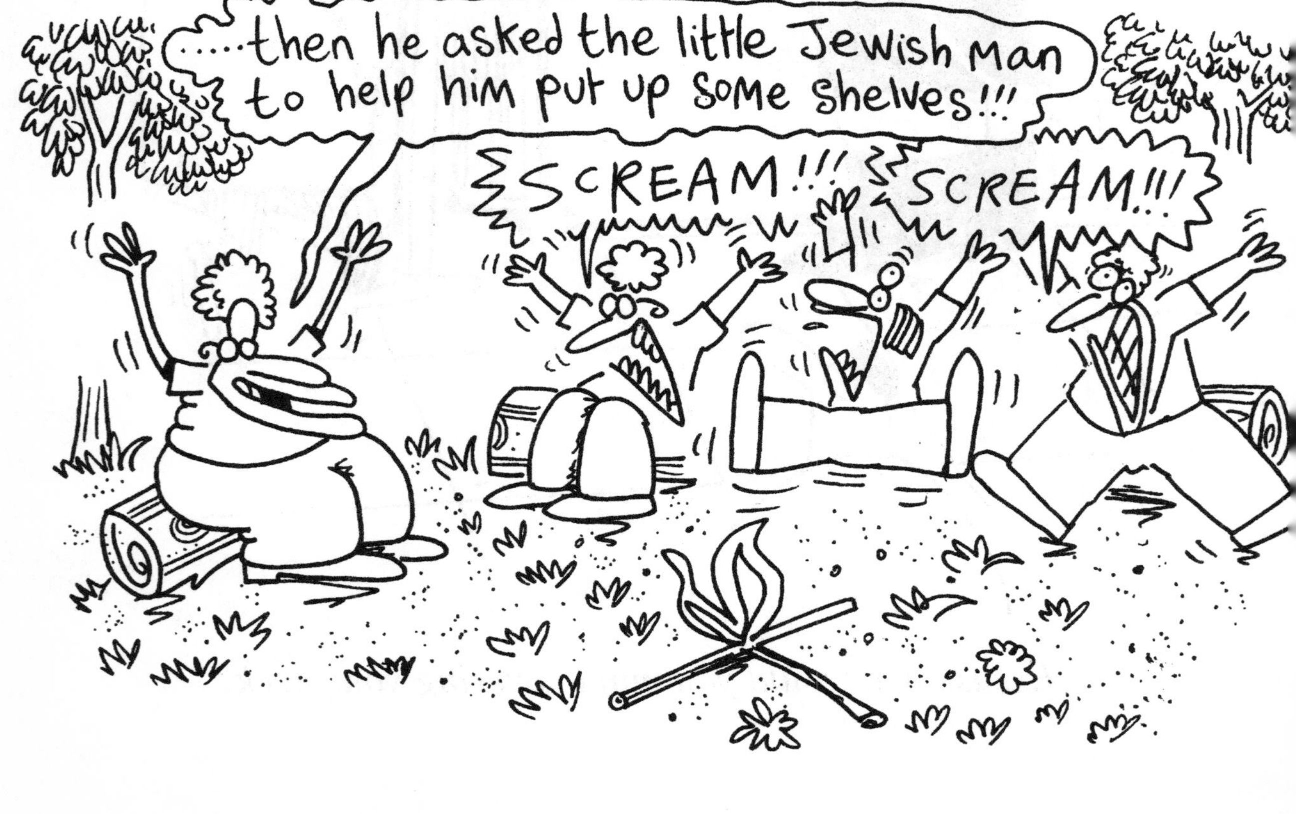

....then he asked the little Jewish man to help him put up some shelves!!!
SCREAM!!!
SCREAM!!!

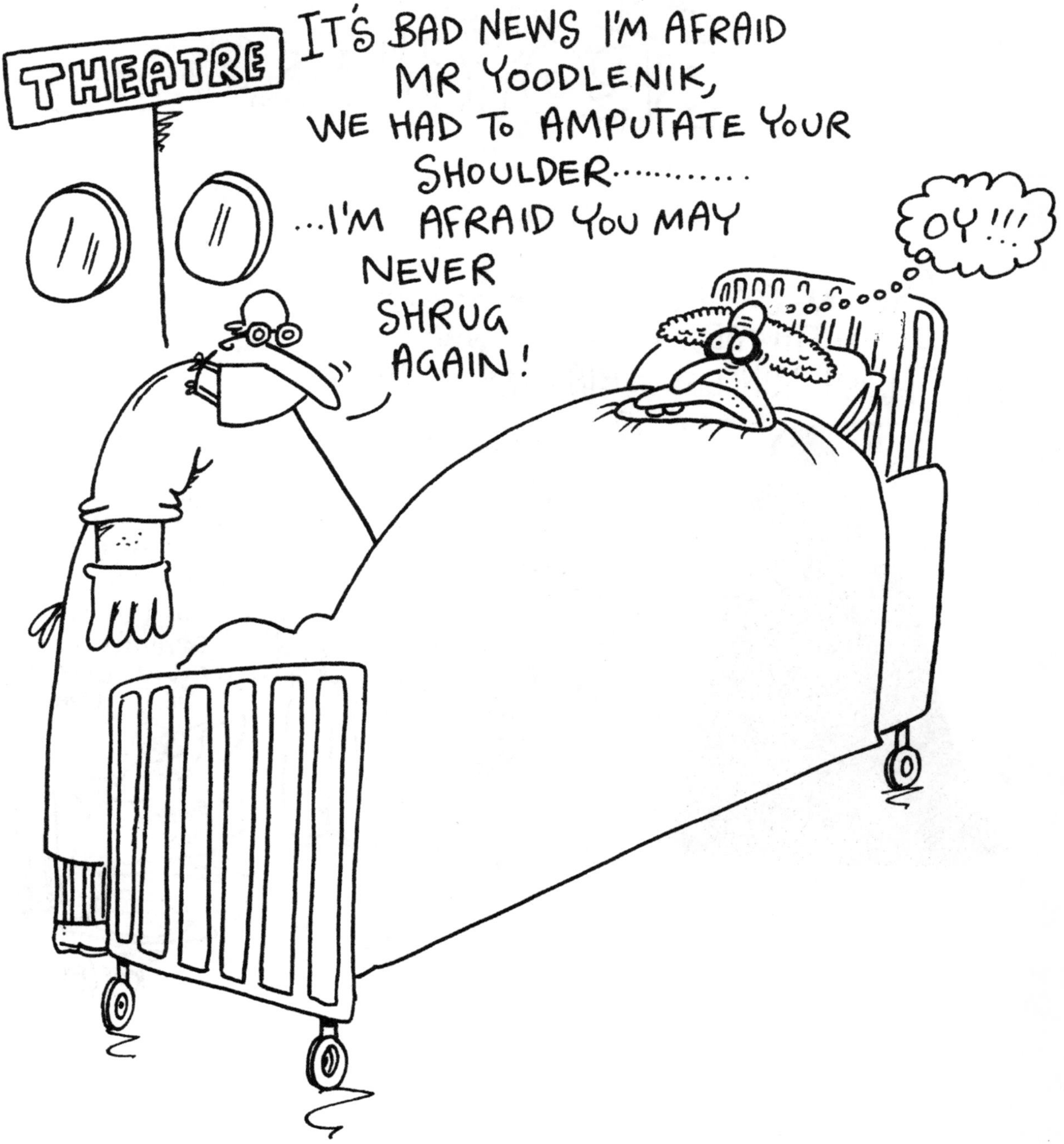
THEATRE
IT'S BAD NEWS I'M AFRAID MR YOODLENIK, WE HAD TO AMPUTATE YOUR SHOULDER.......... ...I'M AFRAID YOU MAY NEVER SHRUG AGAIN!
OY!!!

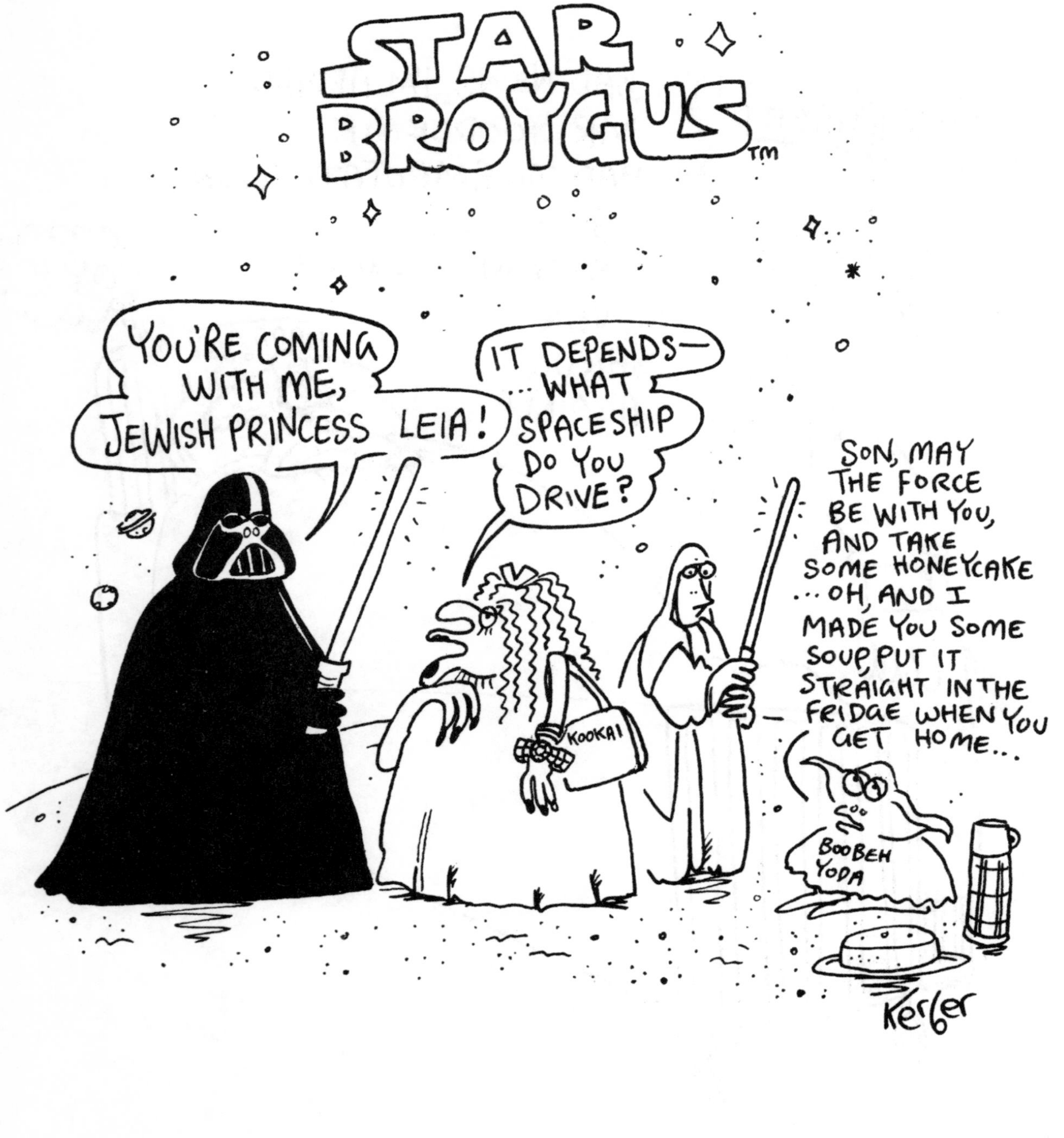
STAR BROYGUS™
YOU'RE COMING WITH ME, JEWISH PRINCESS LEIA!
IT DEPENDS— ...WHAT SPACESHIP DO YOU DRIVE?
SON, MAY THE FORCE BE WITH YOU, AND TAKE SOME HONEYCAKE ...OH, AND I MADE YOU SOME SOUP, PUT IT STRAIGHT IN THE FRIDGE WHEN YOU GET HOME...
KOOKAI
BOOBEH YODA
Kerber

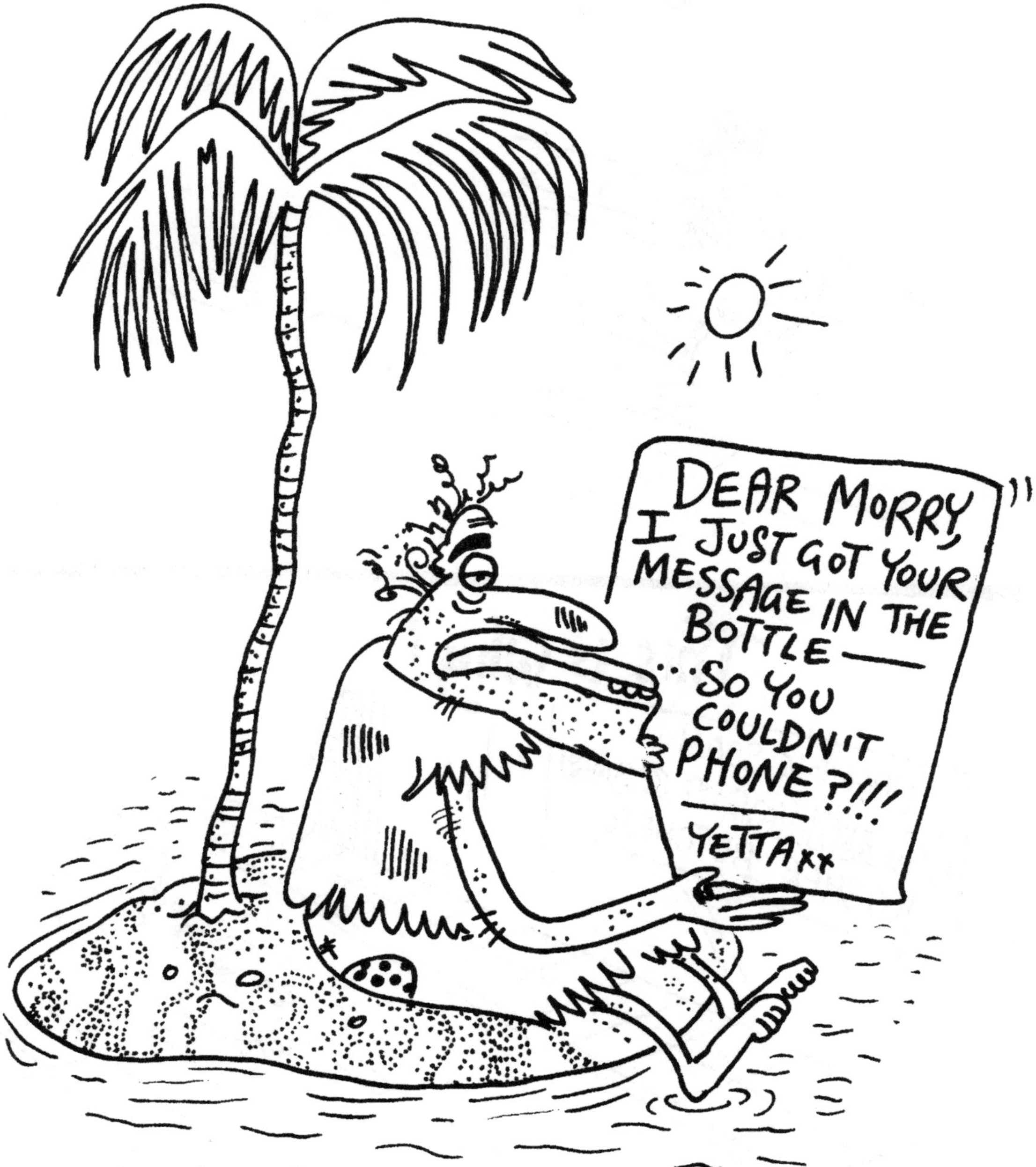
DEAR MORRY,
I JUST GOT YOUR MESSAGE IN THE BOTTLE —
...SO YOU COULDN'T PHONE?!!!
YETTA xx

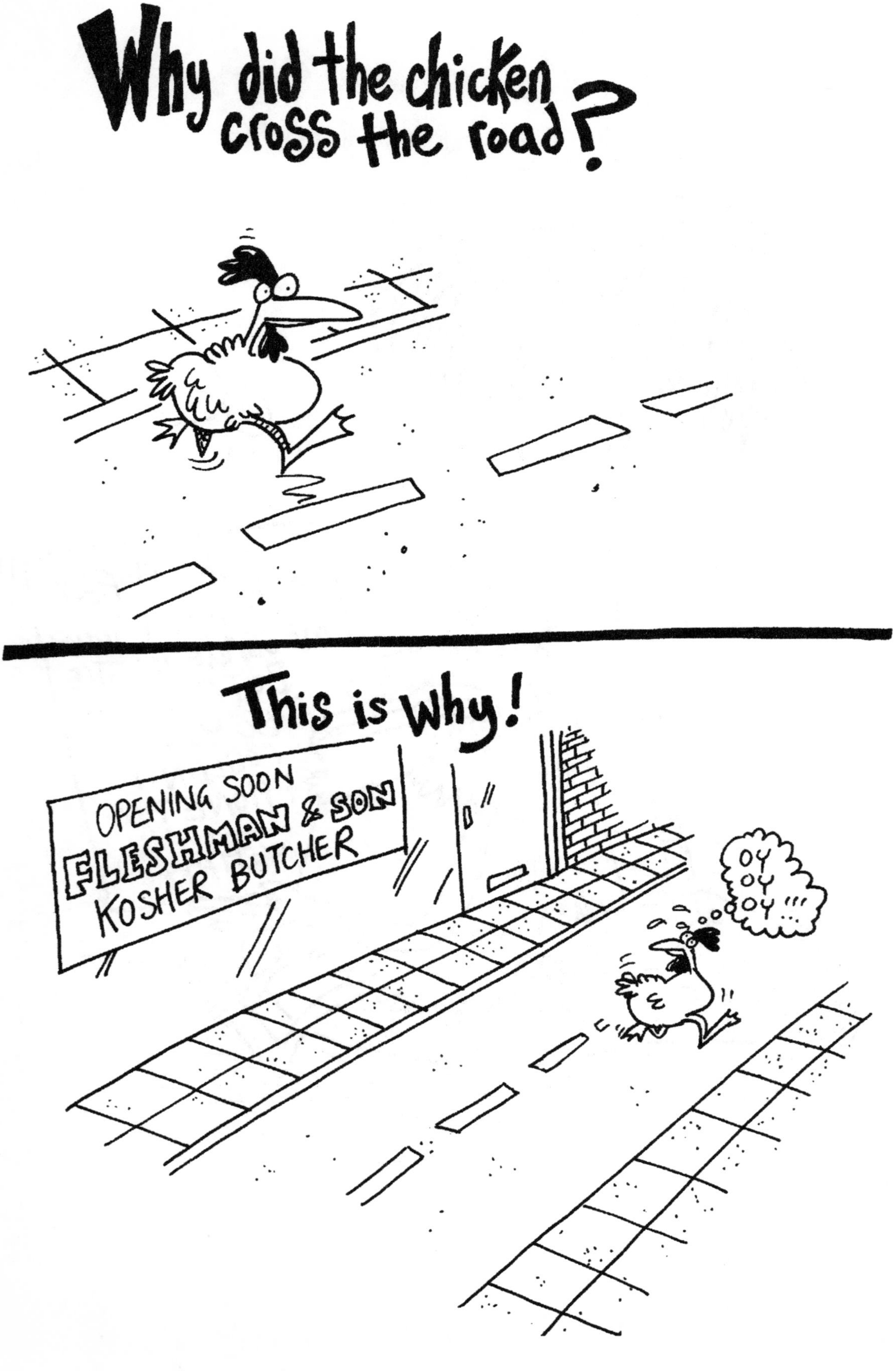
Why did the chicken cross the road?
This is why!
OPENING SOON
FLESHMAN & SON
KOSHER BUTCHER
OY OY OY!!!

JEWISH NOUVELLE CUISINE

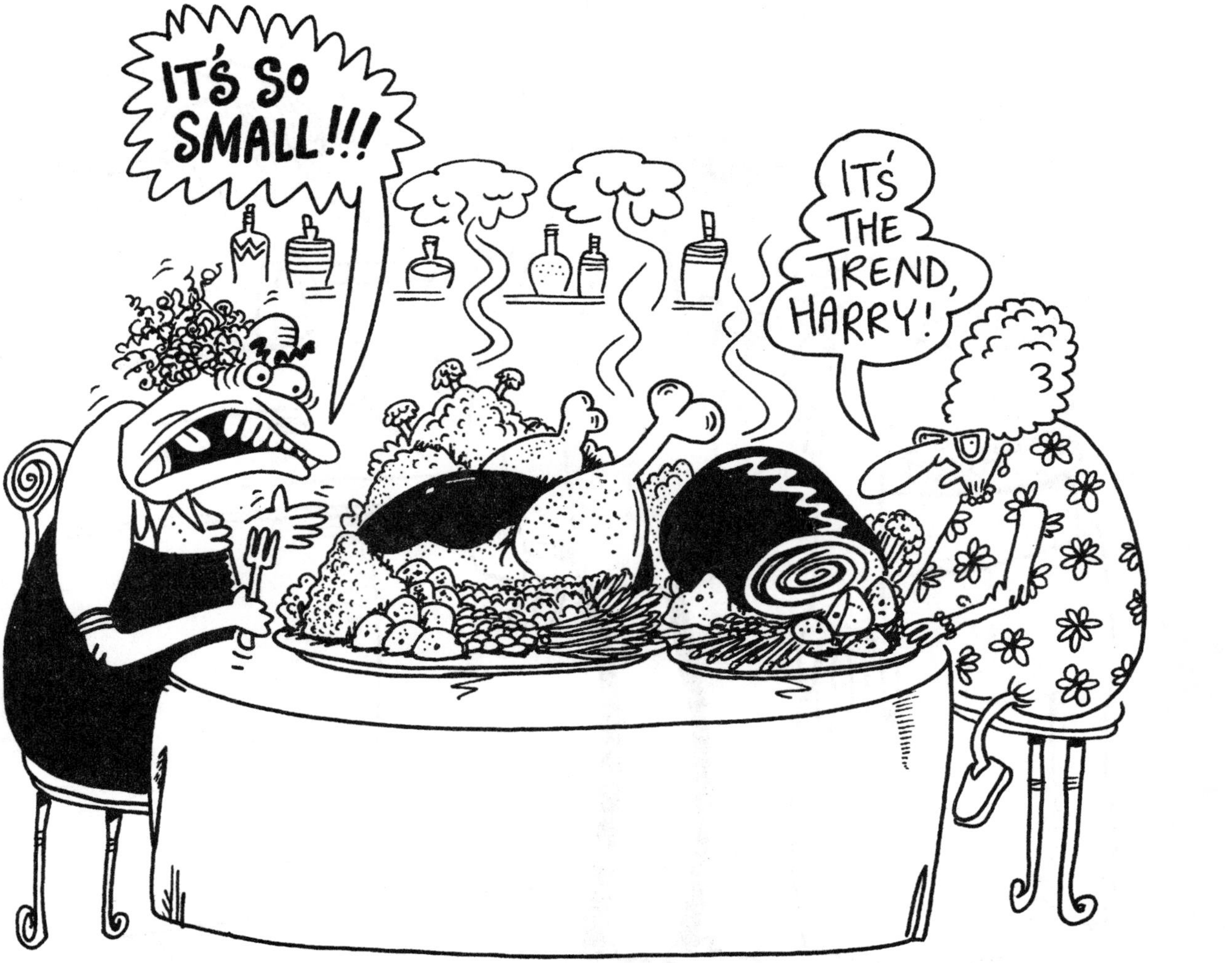

IT'S SO SMALL!!!
IT'S THE TREND, HARRY!

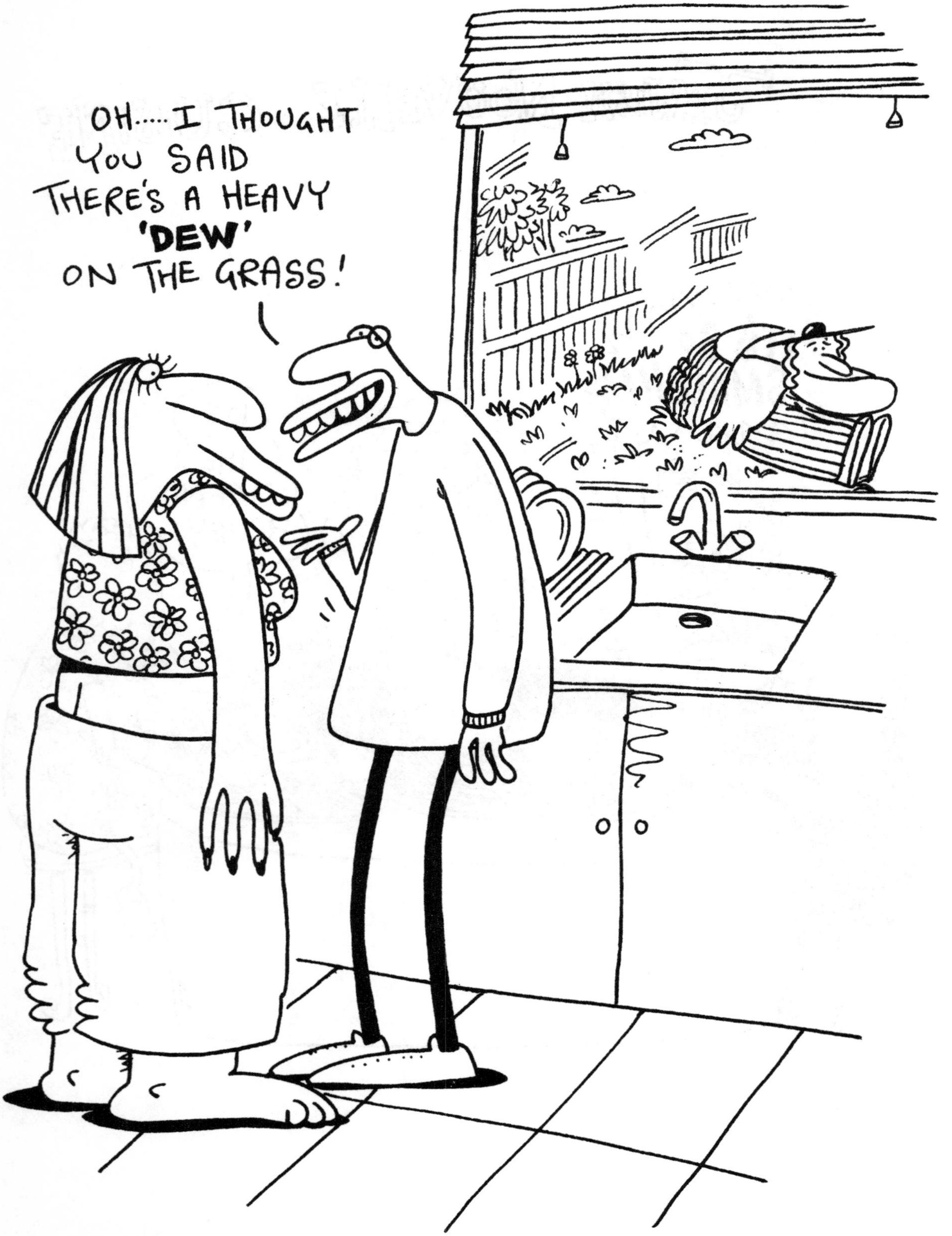
OH..... I THOUGHT YOU SAID THERE'S A HEAVY 'DEW' ON THE GRASS!

THE CHOSEN

EPISODE 8

OVERWORKED AND TIRED FROM ALL THE ATTENTION, MOSES UNWITTINGLY MIXED UP HIS **COMMANDMENTS** WITH HIS **COMMANDS,**

.....MANAGING TO GET THE CHILDREN OF ISRAEL TO "SIT," BUT HAVING TROUBLE TEACHING HIS DOG THAT "THOU SHALT NOT STEAL"

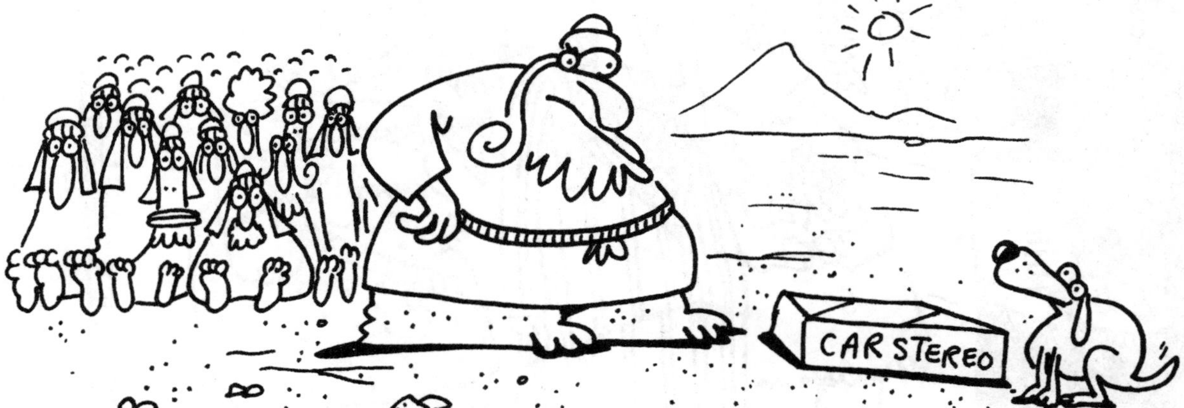

CAR STEREO

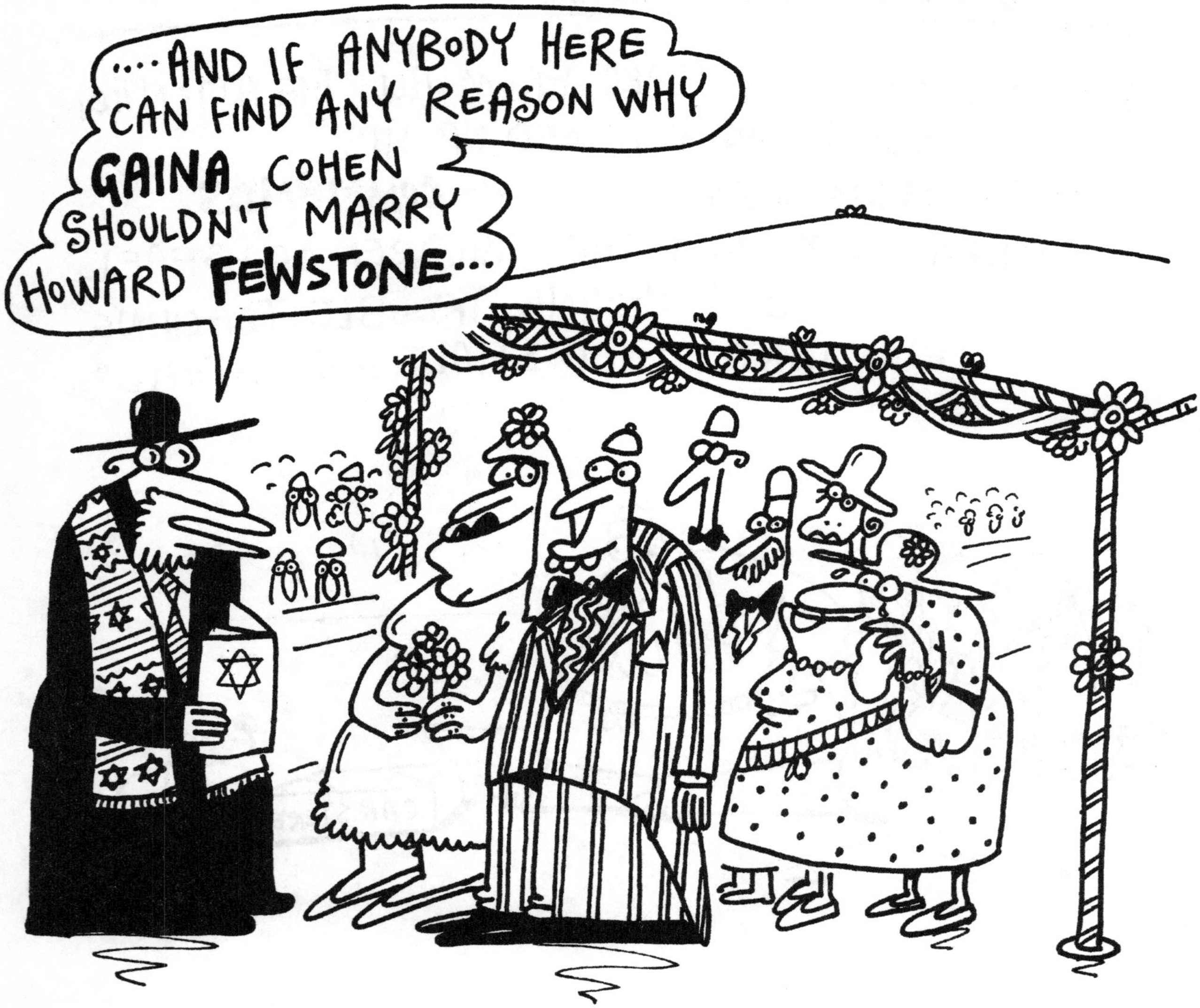
....AND IF ANYBODY HERE CAN FIND ANY REASON WHY GAINA COHEN SHOULDN'T MARRY HOWARD FEWSTONE...

Although never really spoken about, Cupids' Mother was in fact Jewish.

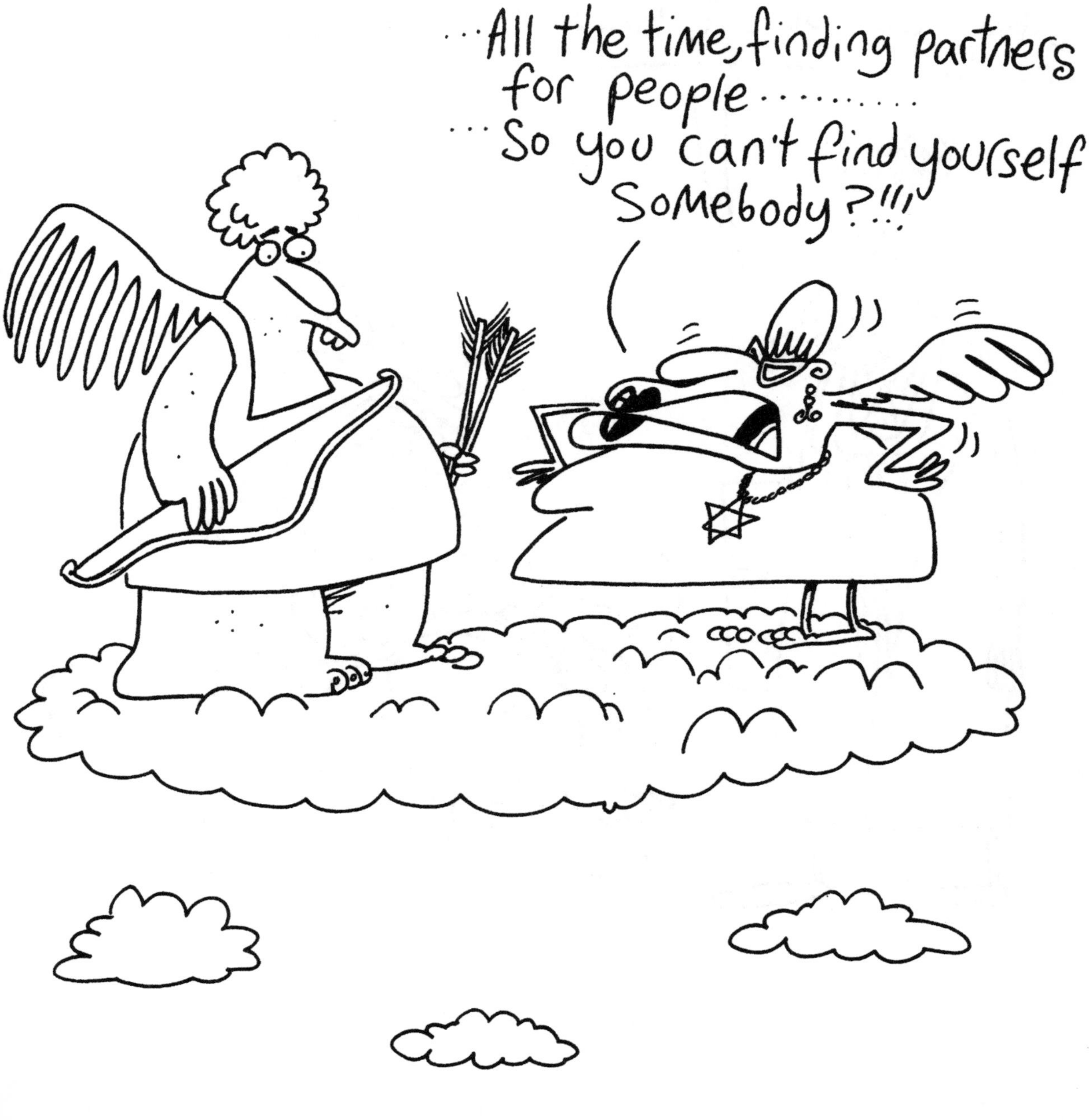
...All the time, finding partners for people.........
...So you can't find yourself Somebody?!!!

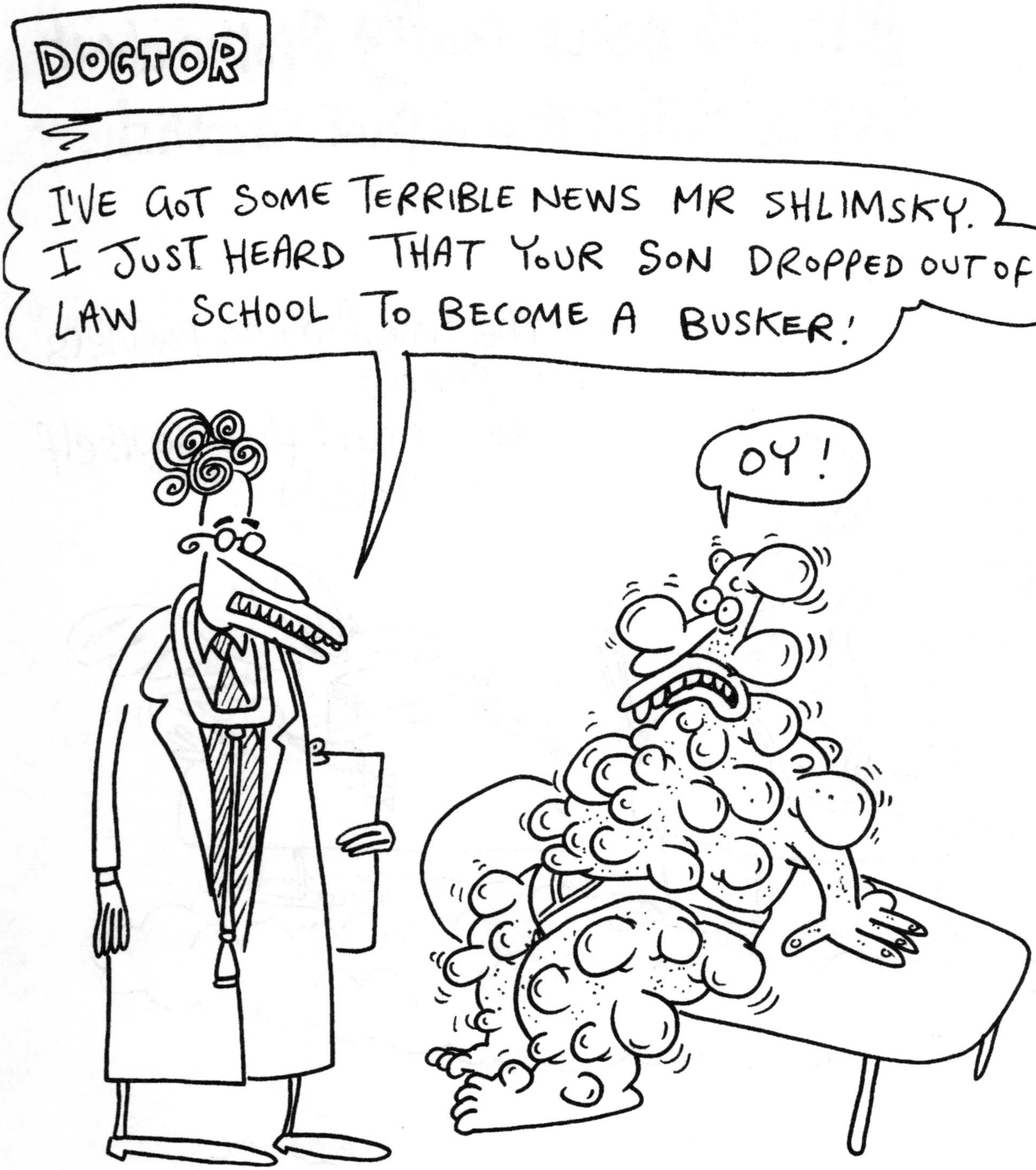
DOCTOR
I'VE GOT SOME TERRIBLE NEWS MR SHLIMSKY. I JUST HEARD THAT YOUR SON DROPPED OUT OF LAW SCHOOL TO BECOME A BUSKER!
OY!

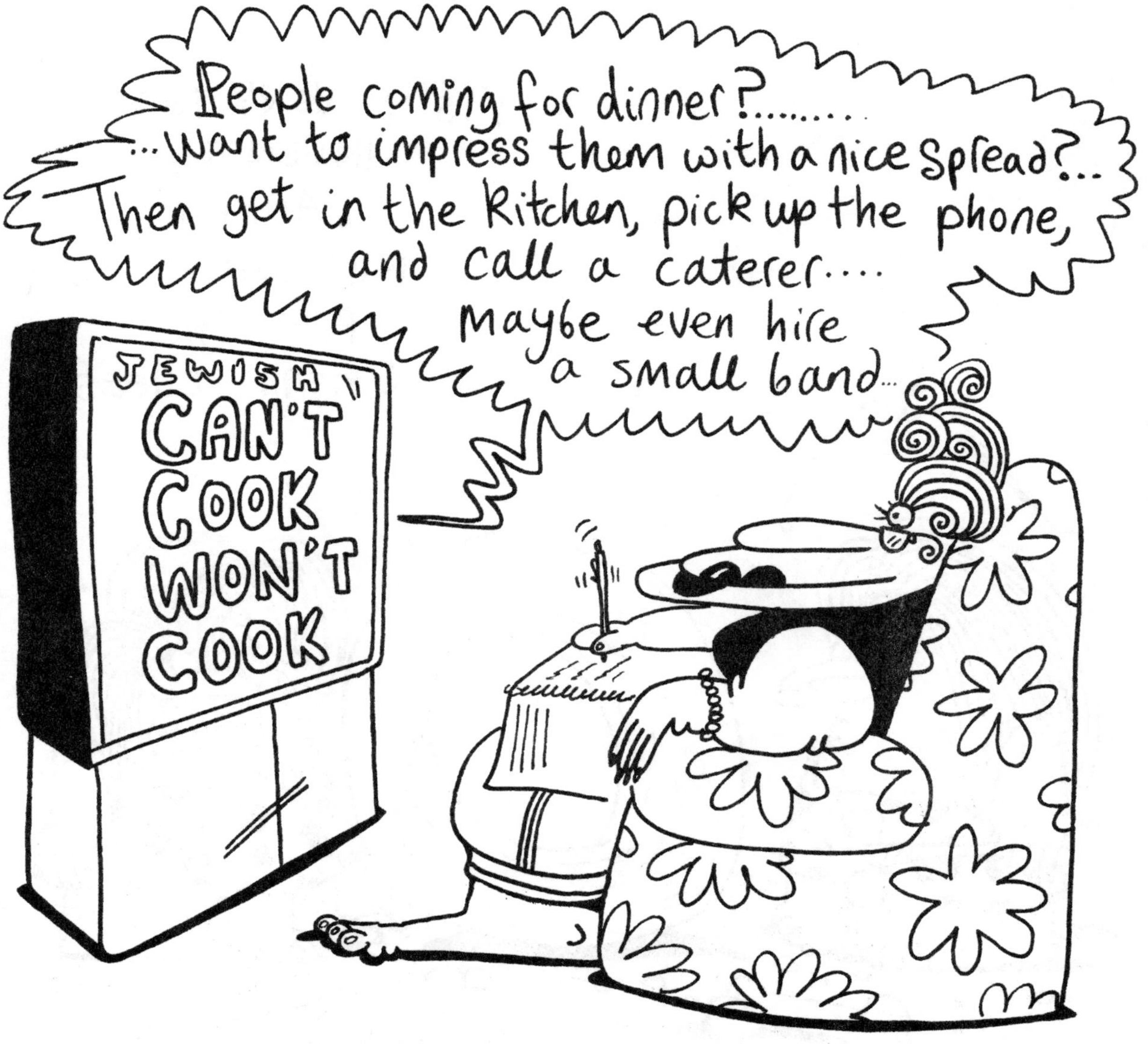
People coming for dinner?........
...want to impress them with a nice spread?...
Then get in the kitchen, pick up the phone, and call a caterer....
maybe even hire a small band...
JEWISH "CAN'T COOK WON'T COOK"

The Cavemans

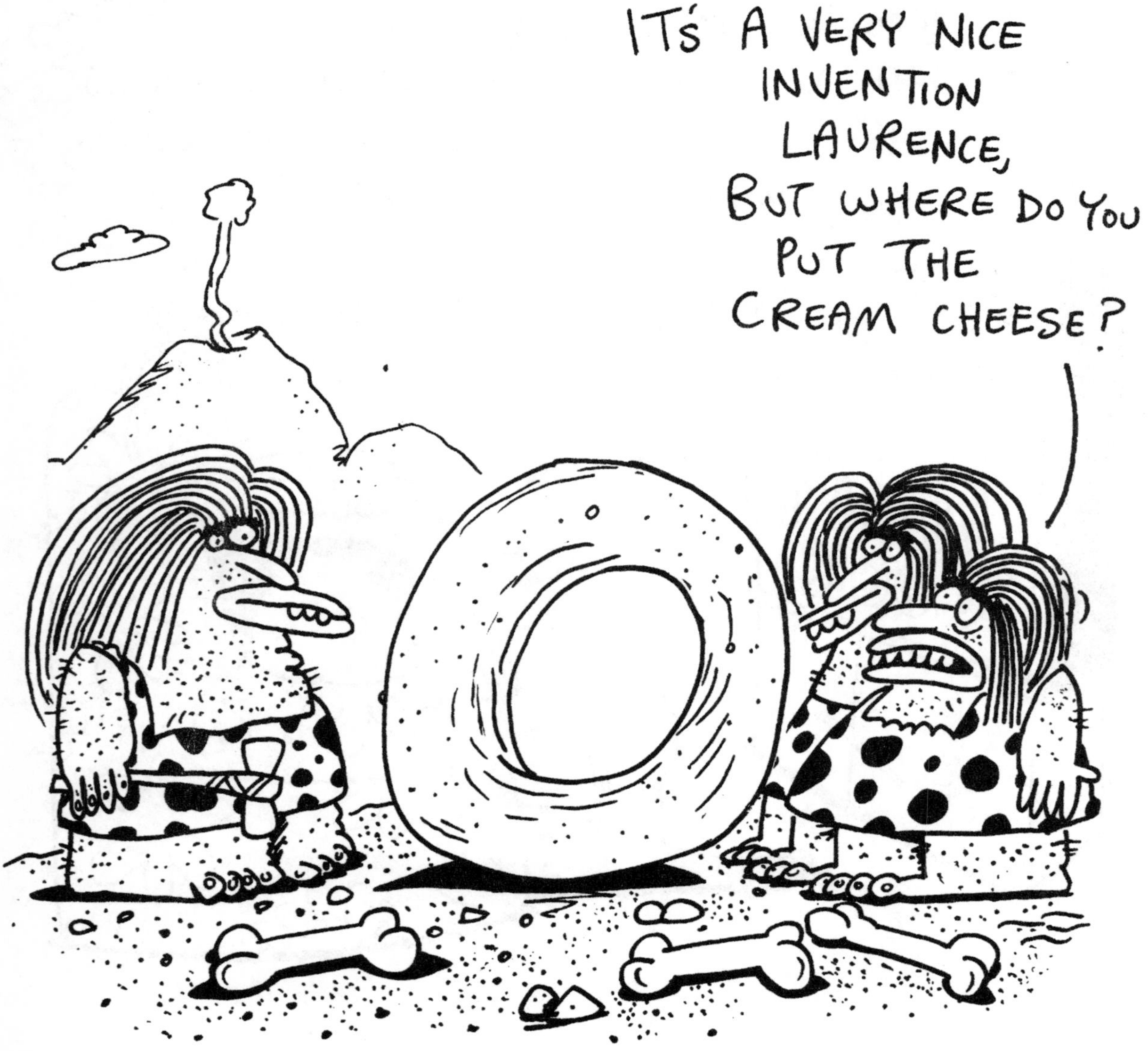
IT'S A VERY NICE INVENTION LAURENCE, BUT WHERE DO YOU PUT THE CREAM CHEESE?

2 Million B.J.
(BEFORE JEWS)

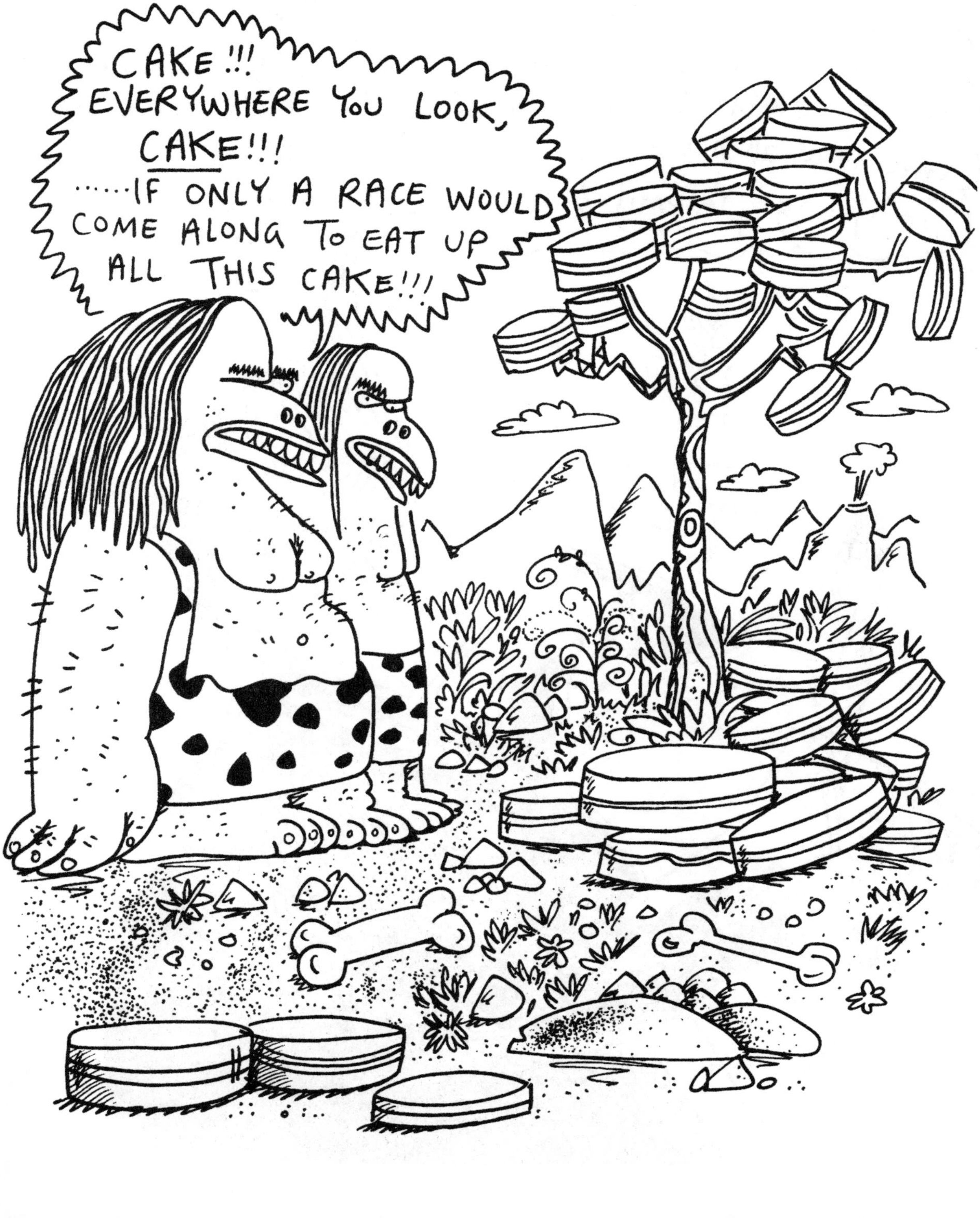
CAKE!!!
EVERYWHERE YOU LOOK, CAKE!!!
.....IF ONLY A RACE WOULD COME ALONG TO EAT UP ALL THIS CAKE!!!

BEFORE BECOMING A SUCCESSFUL PLAYWRIGHT, WILLIAM SHAKESPEARE BEGAN HIS CAREER WRITING BAR-MITZVAH SPEECHES.....

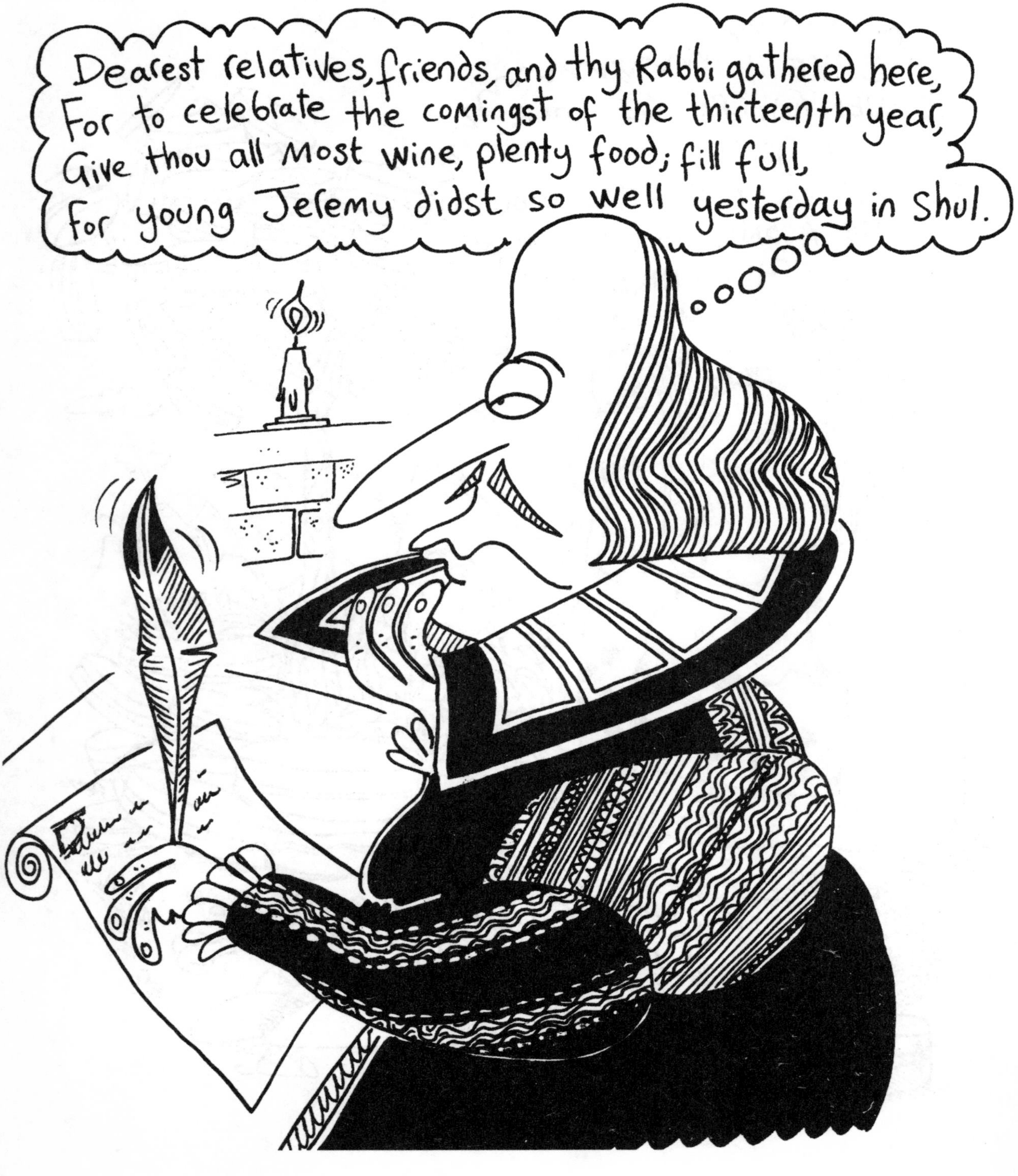
Dearest relatives, friends, and thy Rabbi gathered here,
For to celebrate the comingst of the thirteenth year,
Give thou all most wine, plenty food; fill full,
For young Jeremy didst so well yesterday in Shul.

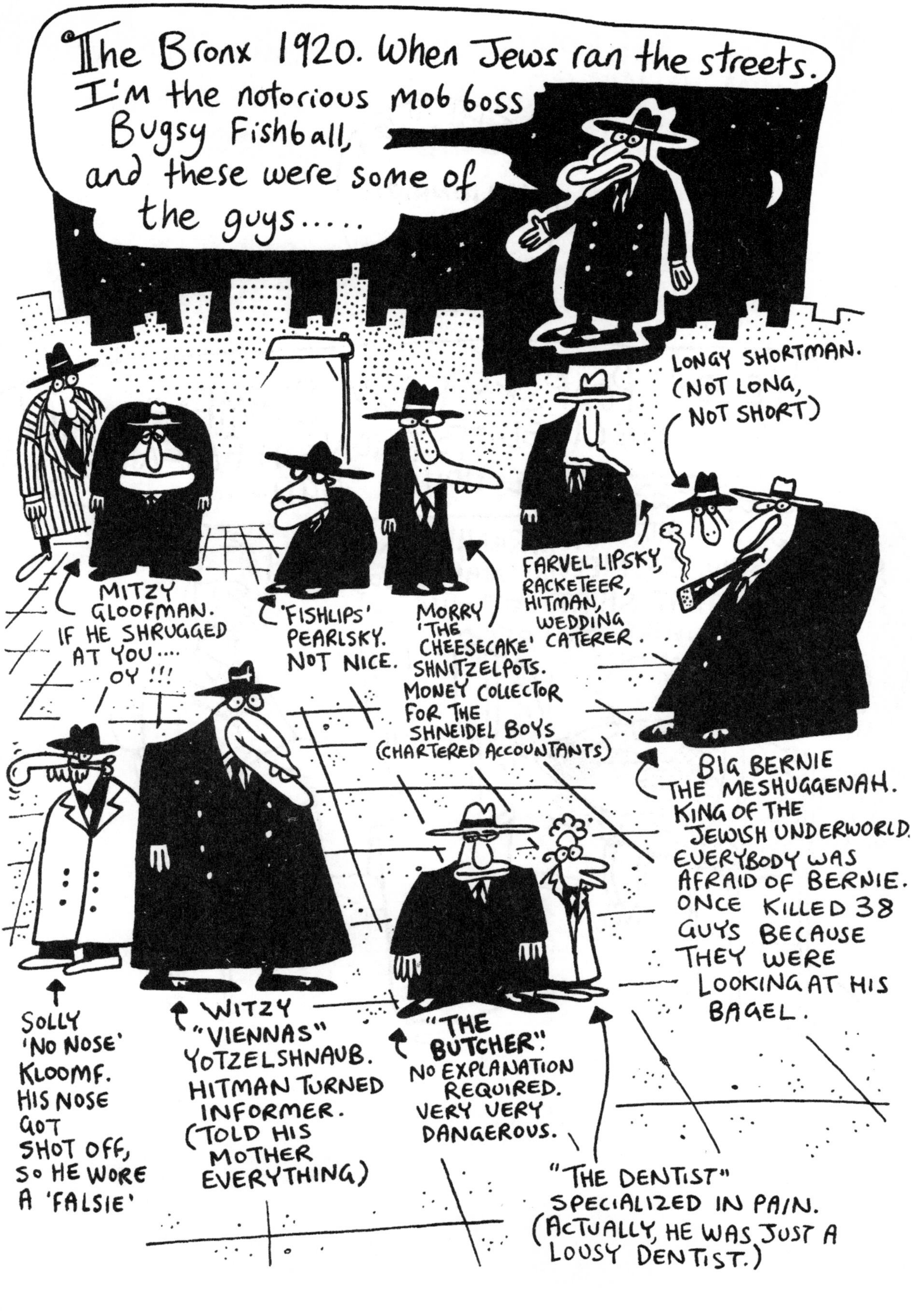
The Bronx 1920. When Jews ran the streets. I'm the notorious mob boss Bugsy Fishball, and these were some of the guys.....
LONGY SHORTMAN. (NOT LONG, NOT SHORT)
MITZY GLOOFMAN. IF HE SHRUGGED AT YOU.... OY !!!
'FISHLIPS' PEARLSKY. NOT NICE.
MORRY 'THE CHEESECAKE' SHNITZELPOTS. MONEY COLLECTOR FOR THE SHNEIDEL BOYS (CHARTERED ACCOUNTANTS)
FARVEL LIPSKY, RACKETEER, HITMAN, WEDDING CATERER.
BIG BERNIE THE MESHUGGENAH. KING OF THE JEWISH UNDERWORLD. EVERYBODY WAS AFRAID OF BERNIE. ONCE KILLED 38 GUYS BECAUSE THEY WERE LOOKING AT HIS BAGEL.
SOLLY 'NO NOSE' KLOOMF. HIS NOSE GOT SHOT OFF, SO HE WORE A 'FALSIE'
WITZY "VIENNAS" YOTZELSHNAUB. HITMAN TURNED INFORMER. (TOLD HIS MOTHER EVERYTHING)
"THE BUTCHER". NO EXPLANATION REQUIRED. VERY VERY DANGEROUS.
"THE DENTIST" SPECIALIZED IN PAIN. (ACTUALLY, HE WAS JUST A LOUSY DENTIST.)

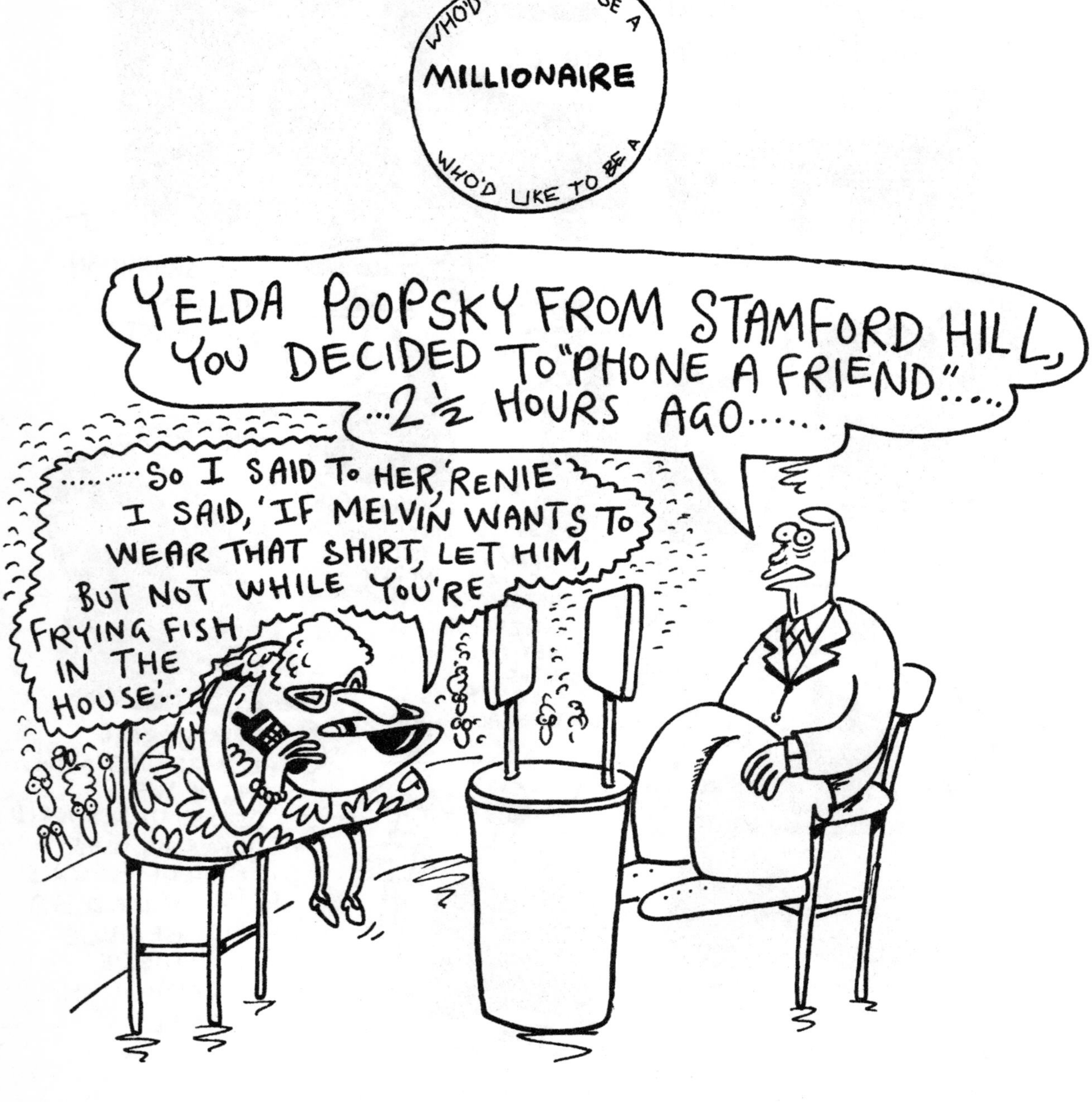
WHO'D LIKE TO BE A MILLIONAIRE WHO'D LIKE TO BE A
YELDA POOPSKY FROM STAMFORD HILL, YOU DECIDED TO "PHONE A FRIEND"..... ...2½ HOURS AGO......
.......SO I SAID TO HER, 'RENIE' I SAID, 'IF MELVIN WANTS TO WEAR THAT SHIRT, LET HIM, BUT NOT WHILE YOU'RE FRYING FISH IN THE HOUSE'..

A SCARY JEWISH HALLOWEEN TALE...

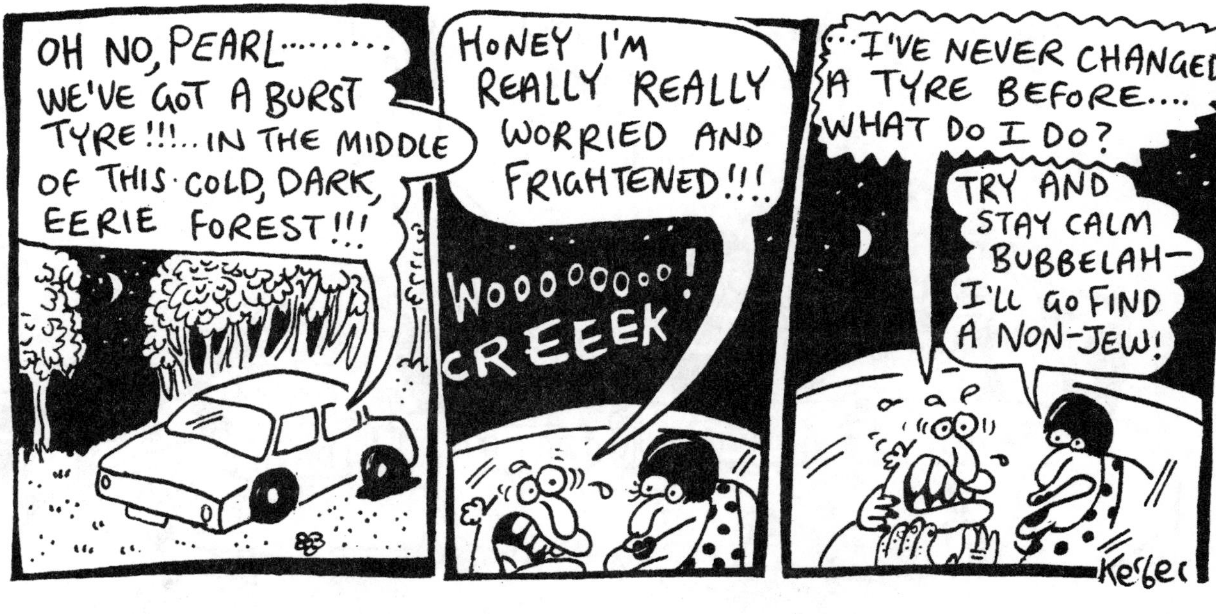
OH NO, PEARL......... WE'VE GOT A BURST TYRE!!!...IN THE MIDDLE OF THIS COLD, DARK, EERIE FOREST!!!
HONEY I'M REALLY REALLY WORRIED AND FRIGHTENED!!!
WOOOOOOOO!
CREEEK
...I'VE NEVER CHANGED A TYRE BEFORE.... WHAT DO I DO?
TRY AND STAY CALM BUBBELAH— I'LL GO FIND A NON-JEW!
Kerber

THE CAMP DAVID AGREEMENT

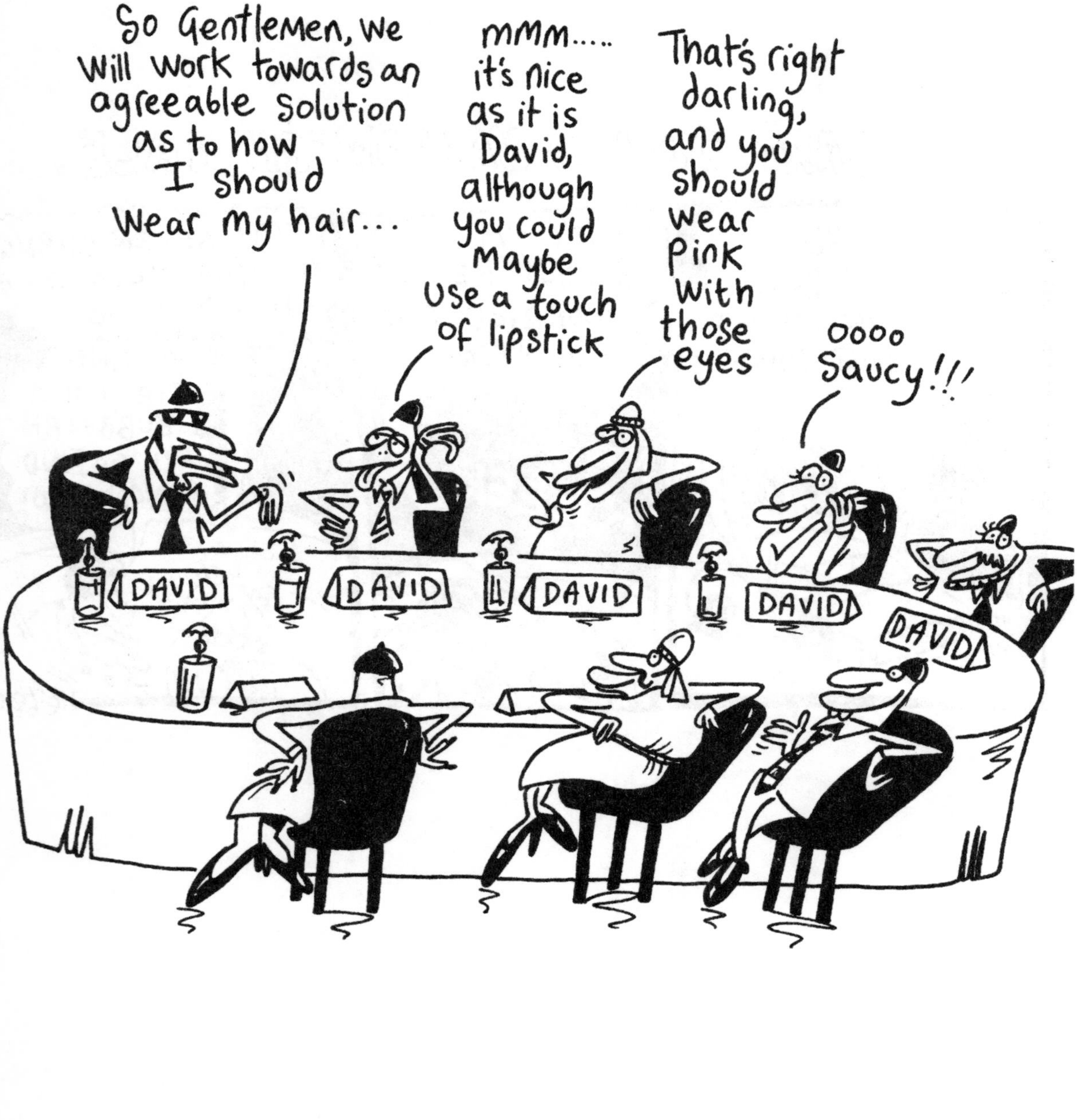
So Gentlemen, we will work towards an agreeable solution as to how I should wear my hair...
mmm..... it's nice as it is David, although you could maybe use a touch of lipstick
That's right darling, and you should wear pink with those eyes
oooo Saucy!!!
DAVID
DAVID
DAVID
DAVID
DAVID

HOW GLOBAL WARMING IS AFFECTING JEWS

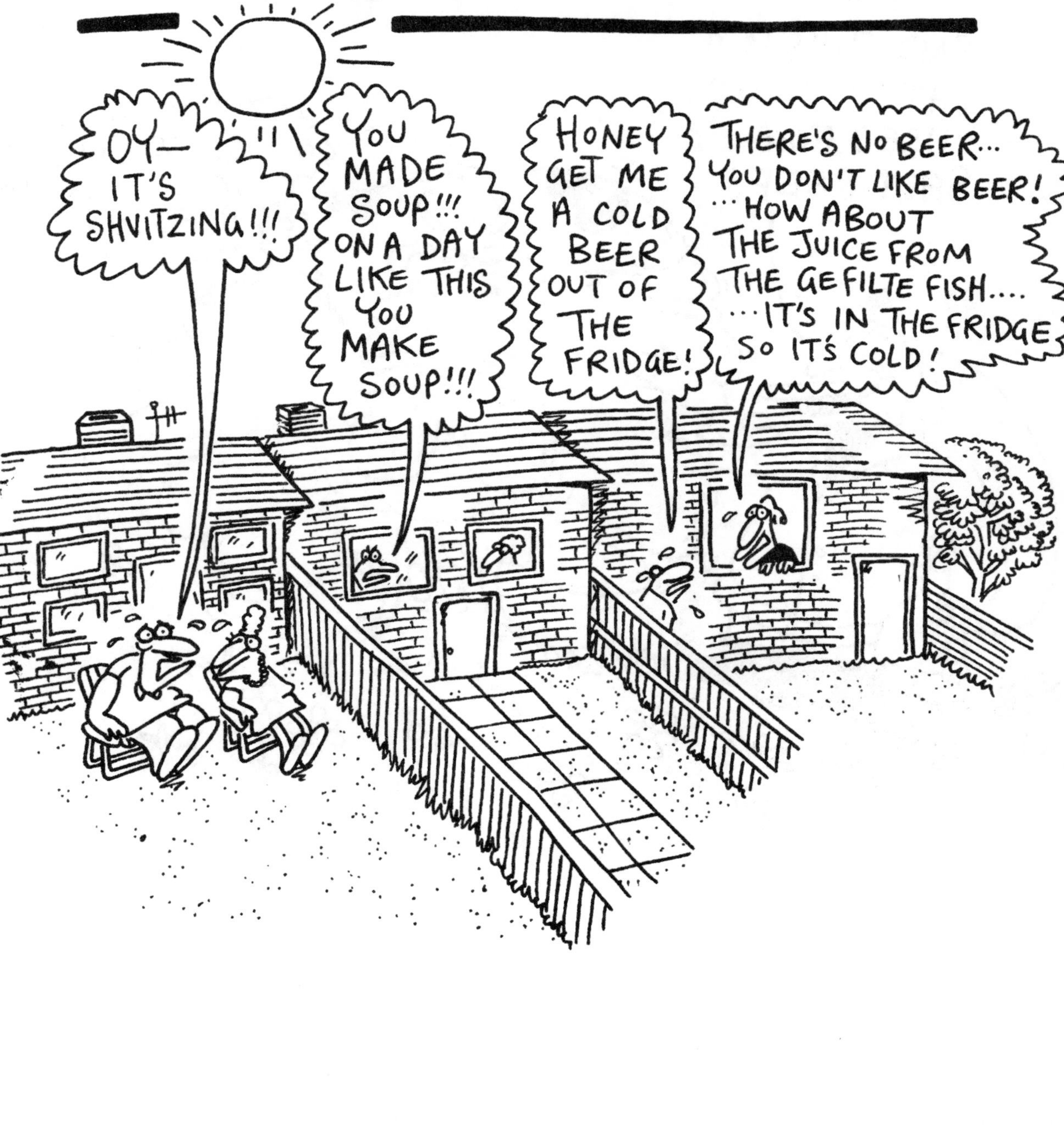
OY— IT'S SHVITZING!!!
YOU MADE SOUP!!! ON A DAY LIKE THIS YOU MAKE SOUP!!!
HONEY GET ME A COLD BEER OUT OF THE FRIDGE!
THERE'S NO BEER... YOU DON'T LIKE BEER! ...HOW ABOUT THE JUICE FROM THE GEFILTE FISH.... ...IT'S IN THE FRIDGE SO IT'S COLD!

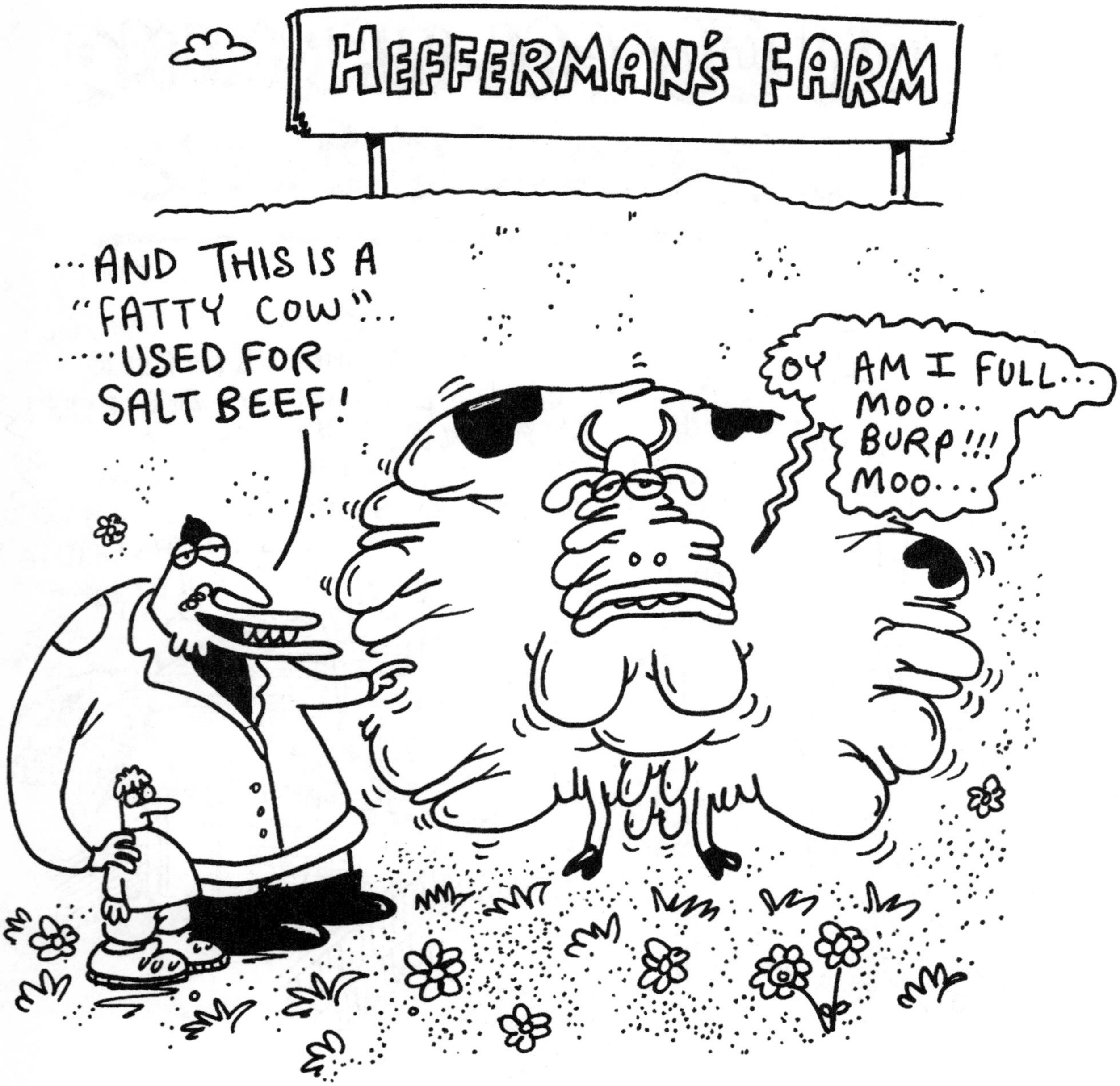
HEFFERMAN'S FARM
...AND THIS IS A "FATTY COW"... ...USED FOR SALT BEEF!
OY AM I FULL... MOO... BURP!!! MOO...

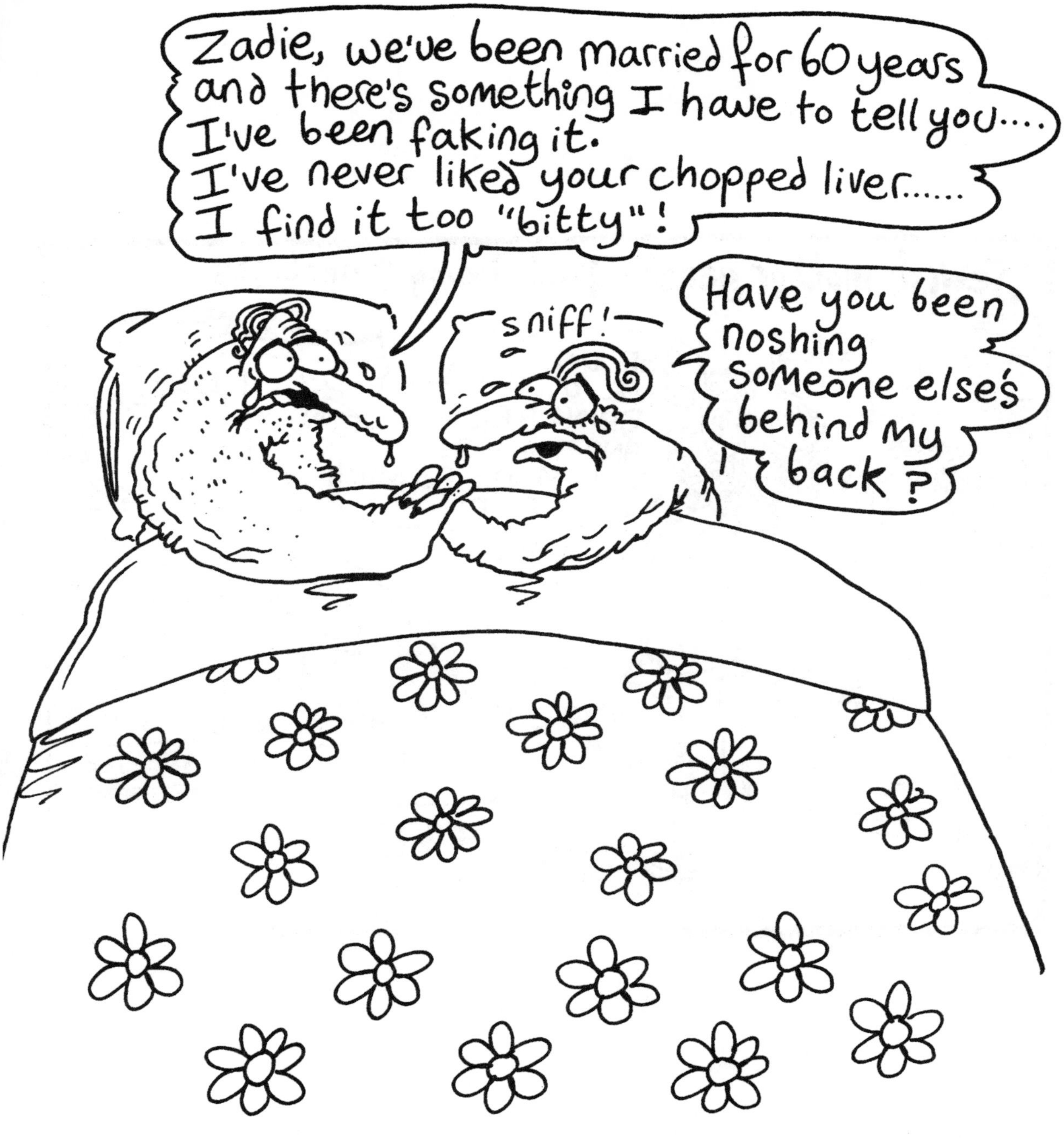
Zadie, we've been married for 60 years and there's something I have to tell you.... I've been faking it. I've never liked your chopped liver...... I find it too "bitty"!
sniff!
Have you been noshing someone else's behind my back?

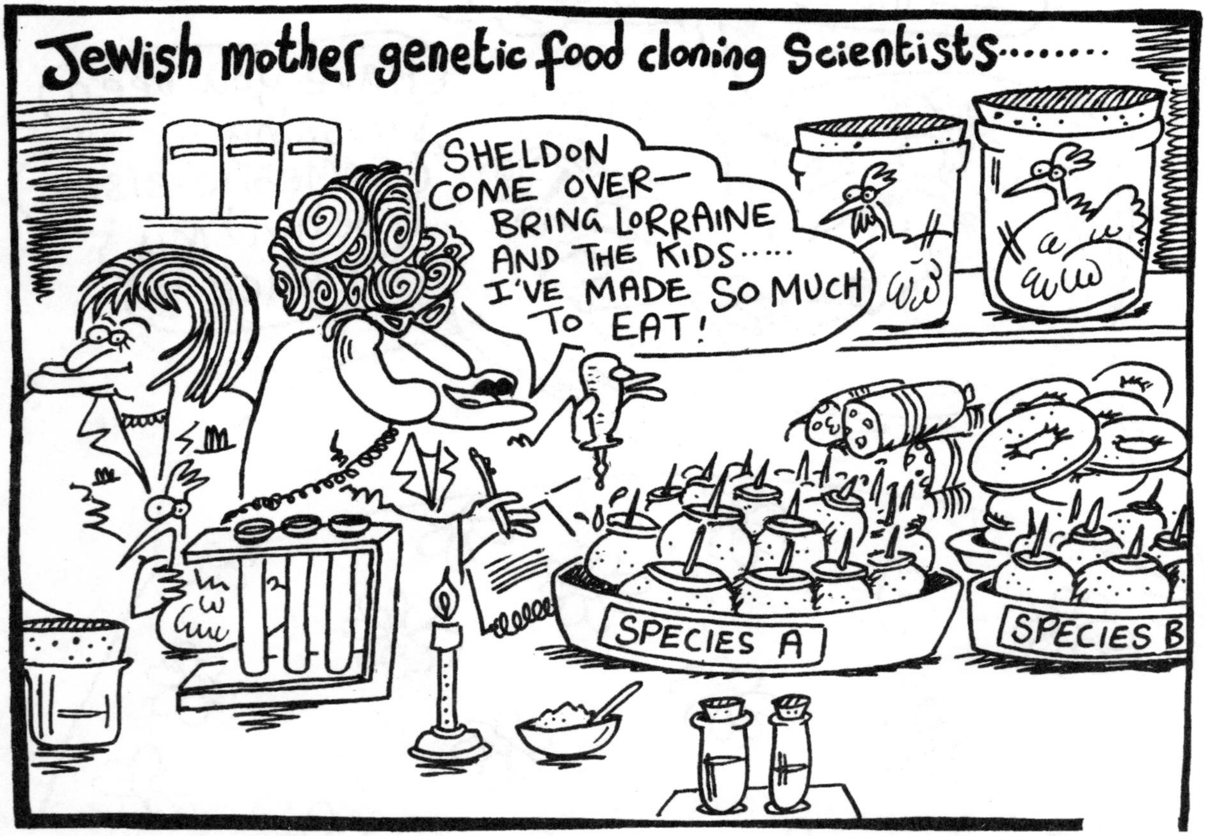
Jewish mother genetic food cloning Scientists.......
SHELDON COME OVER— BRING LORRAINE AND THE KIDS..... I'VE MADE SO MUCH TO EAT!
SPECIES A
SPECIES B

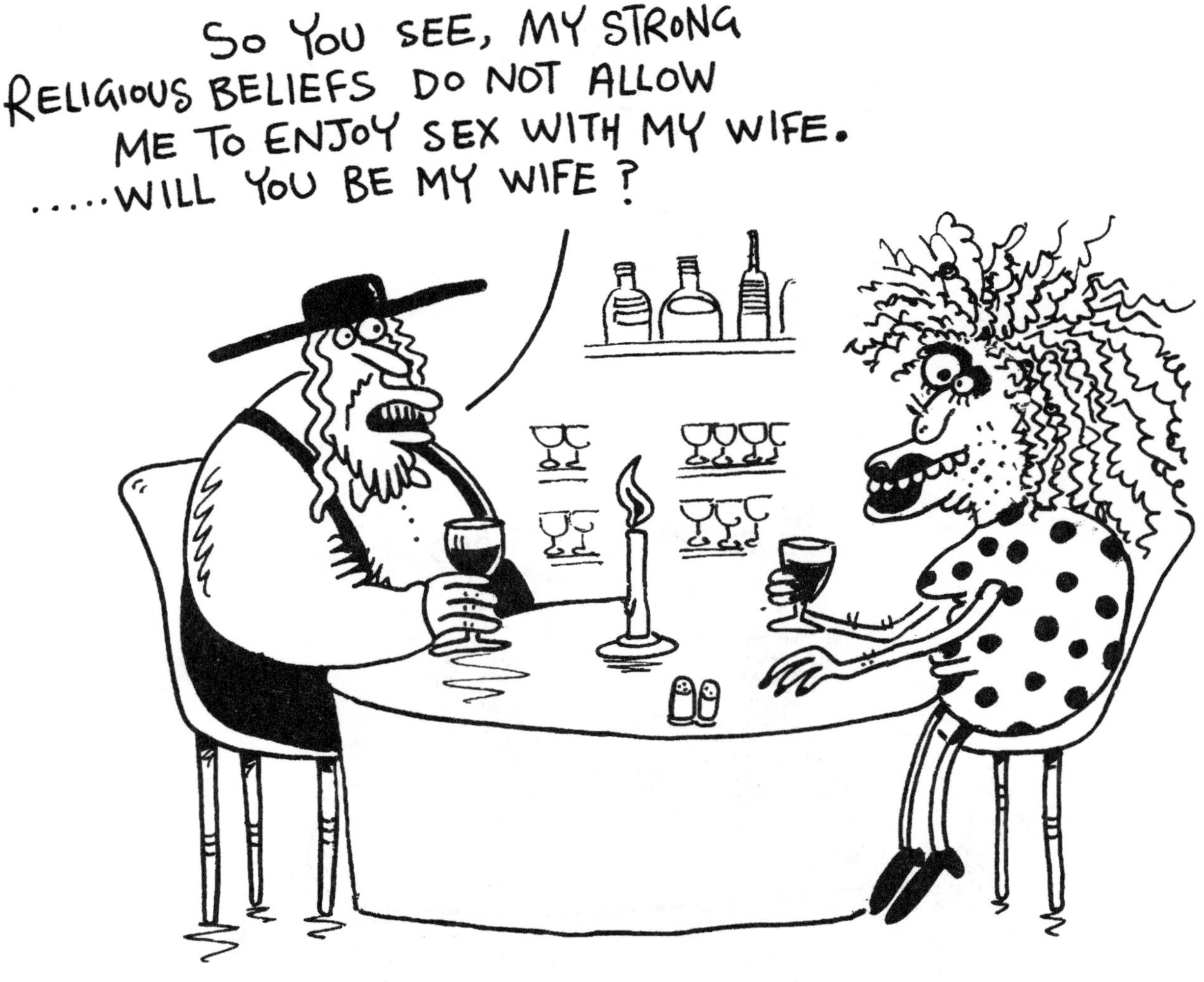
SO YOU SEE, MY STRONG RELIGIOUS BELIEFS DO NOT ALLOW ME TO ENJOY SEX WITH MY WIFE. .....WILL YOU BE MY WIFE ?

2 JEWS, STUCK TOGETHER IN A LIFEBOAT, STRANDED AT SEA......
WHAT WOULD THEY SAY TO EACHOTHER?

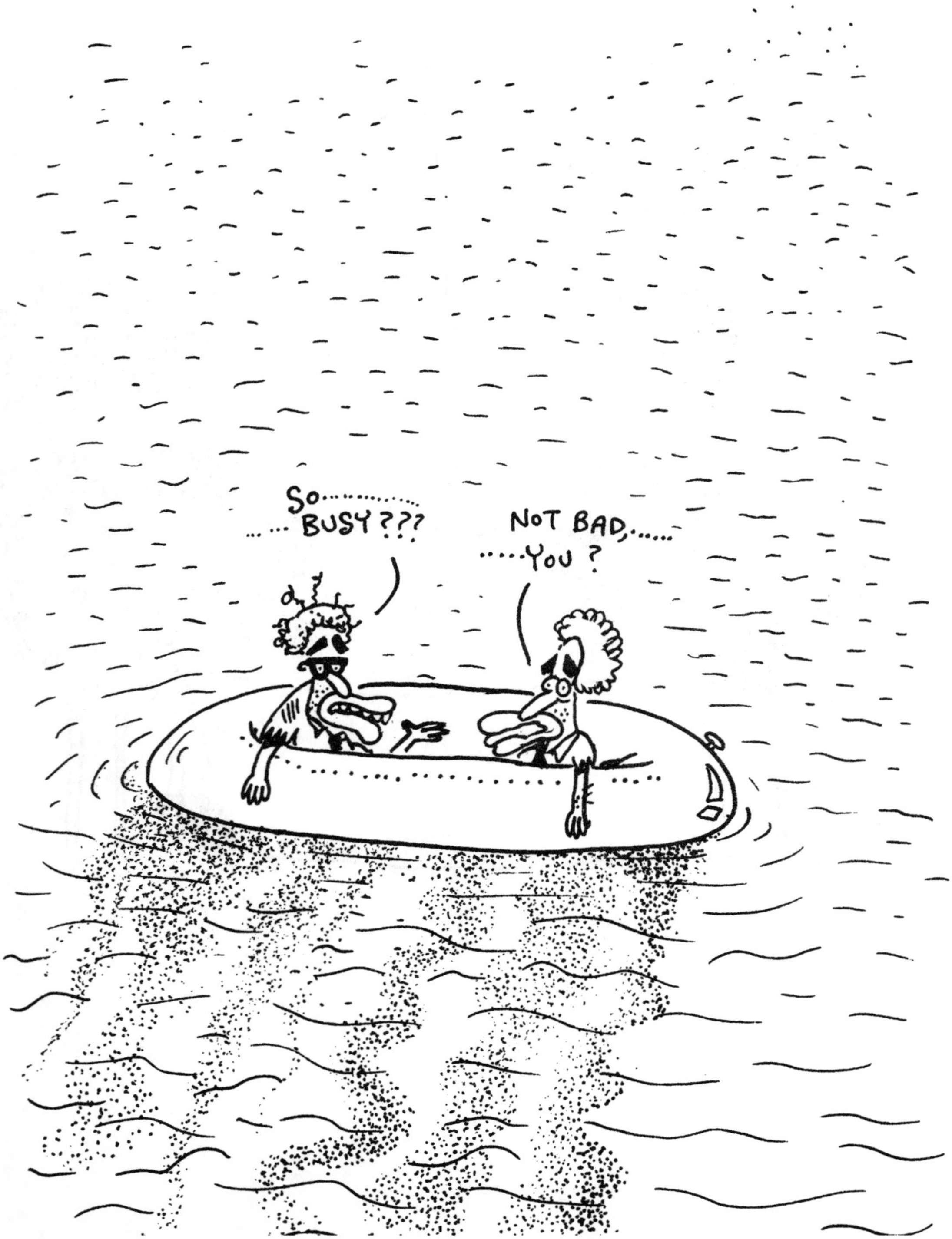
So............
......BUSY???
NOT BAD,......
.....YOU ?

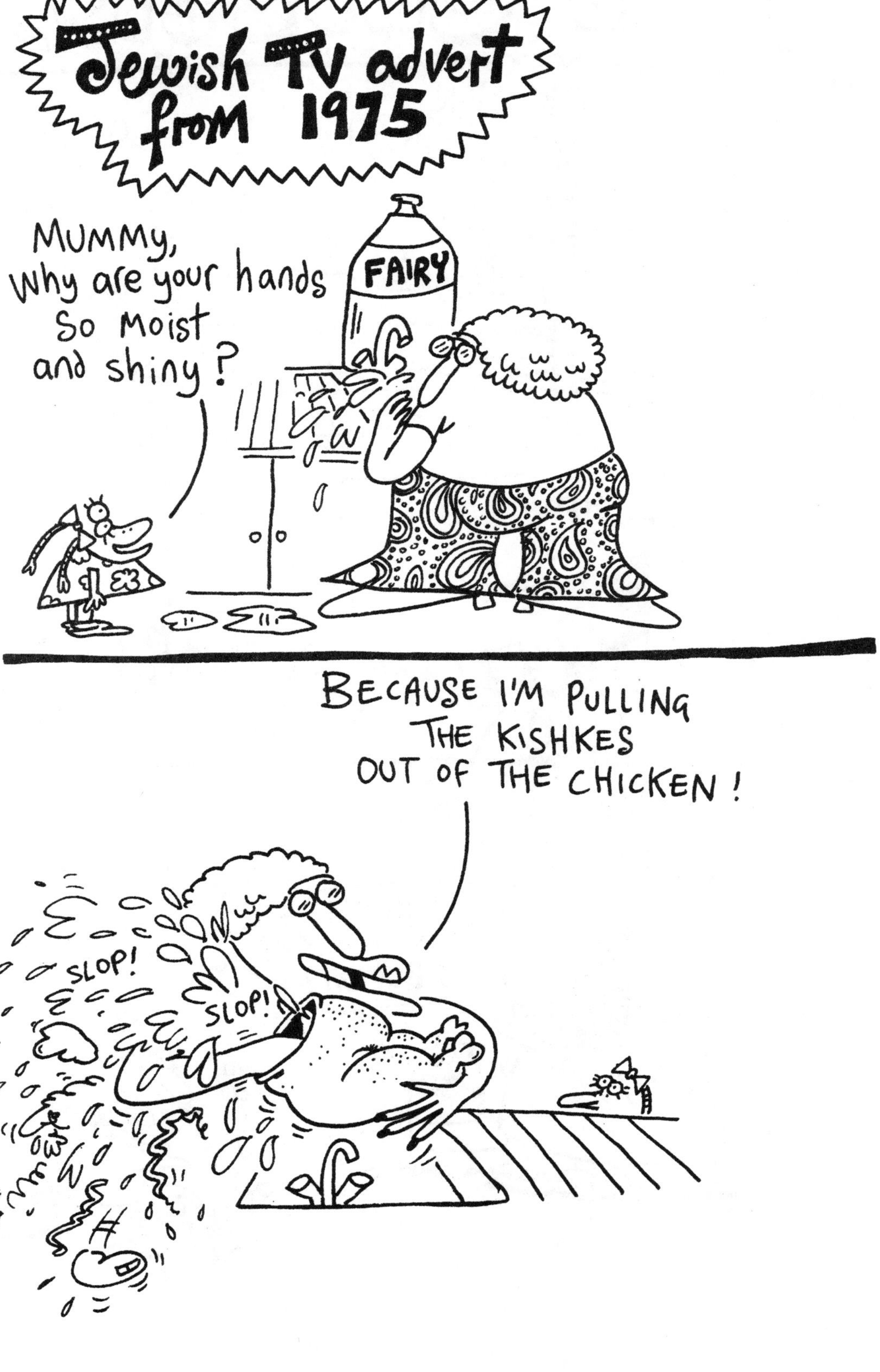
Jewish TV advert from 1975
MUMMY, Why are your hands so moist and shiny?
FAIRY
BECAUSE I'M PULLING THE KISHKES OUT OF THE CHICKEN!
SLOP!
SLOP!

THE CHOSEN

EPISODE 9

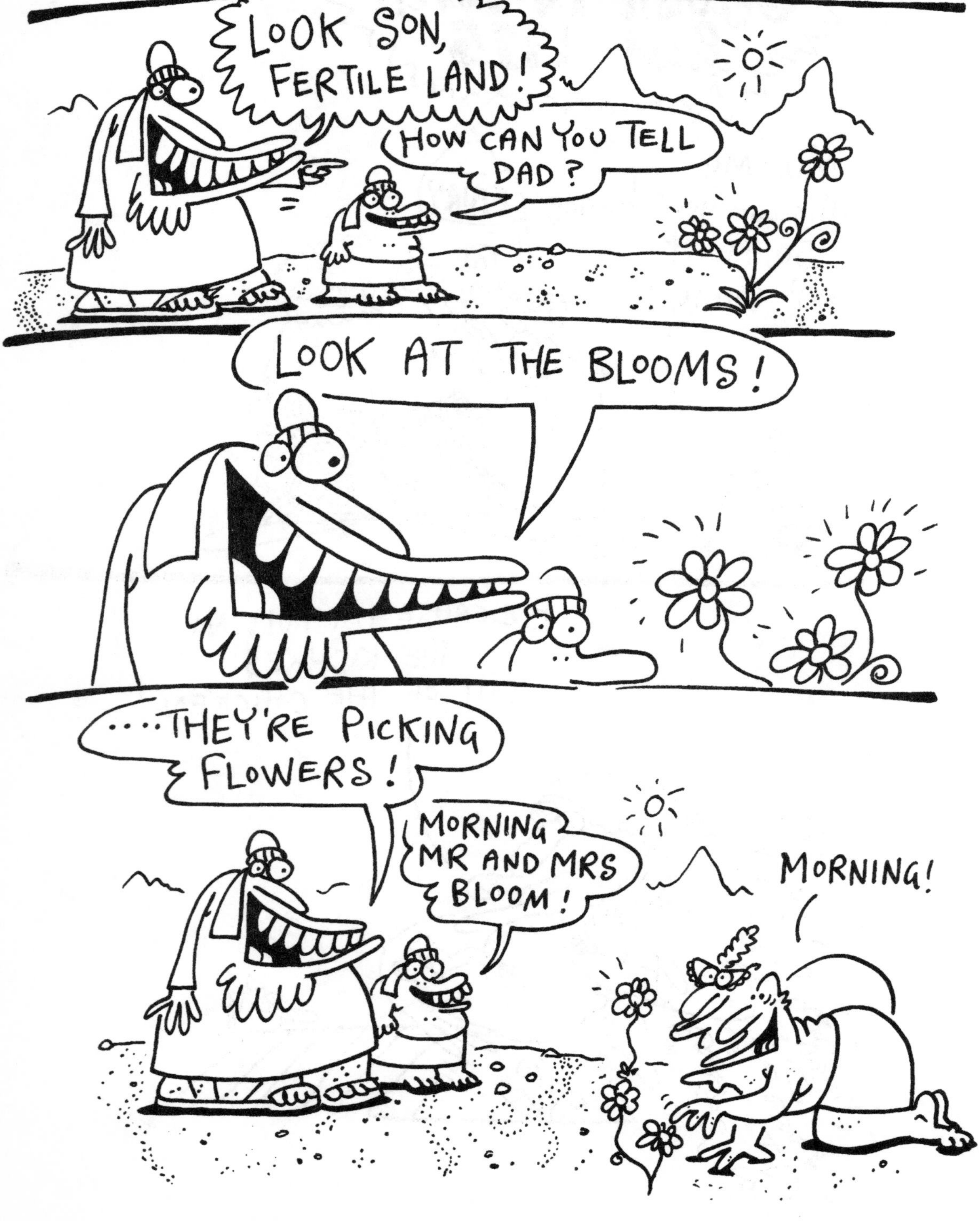

LOOK SON, FERTILE LAND!
HOW CAN YOU TELL DAD?
LOOK AT THE BLOOMS!
....THEY'RE PICKING FLOWERS!
MORNING MR AND MRS BLOOM!
MORNING!

Melvin Pinkel (Jewish clown) GOES HOME TO RELAX

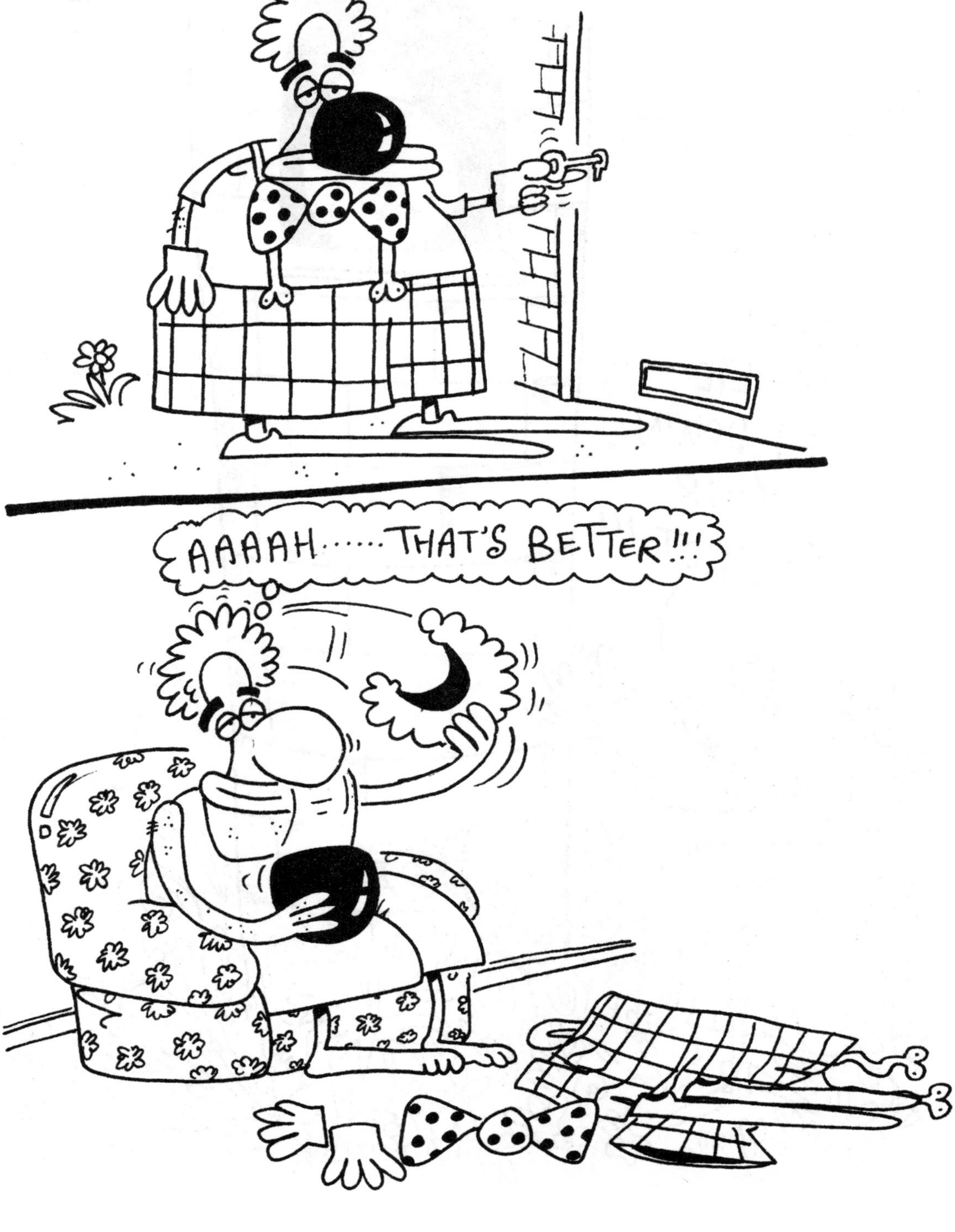
AAAAH ..... THAT'S BETTER!!!

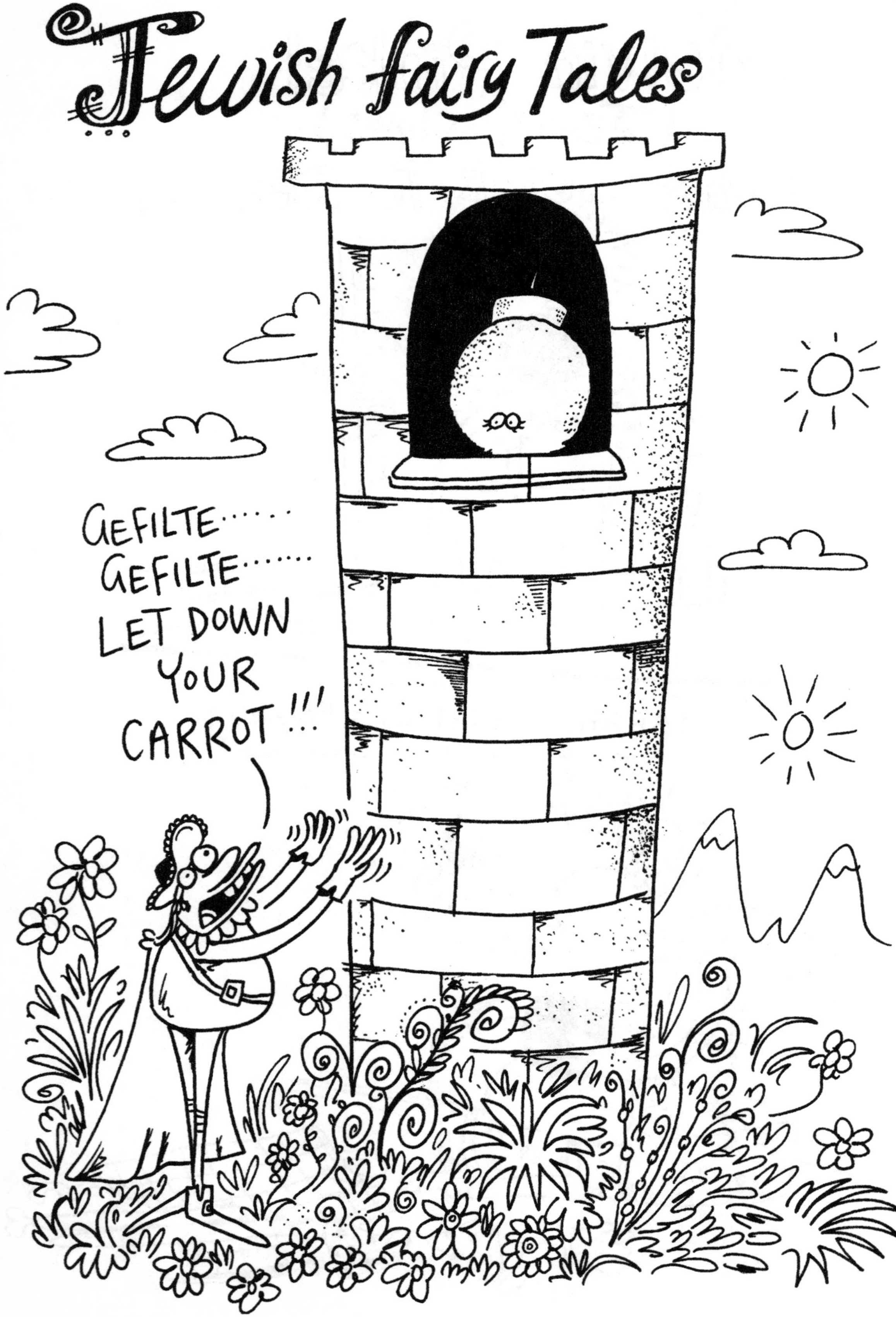
Jewish fairy Tales
GEFILTE......
GEFILTE.......
LET DOWN
YOUR
CARROT!!!

Doctor Dolittle
Shmoozes with the animals...

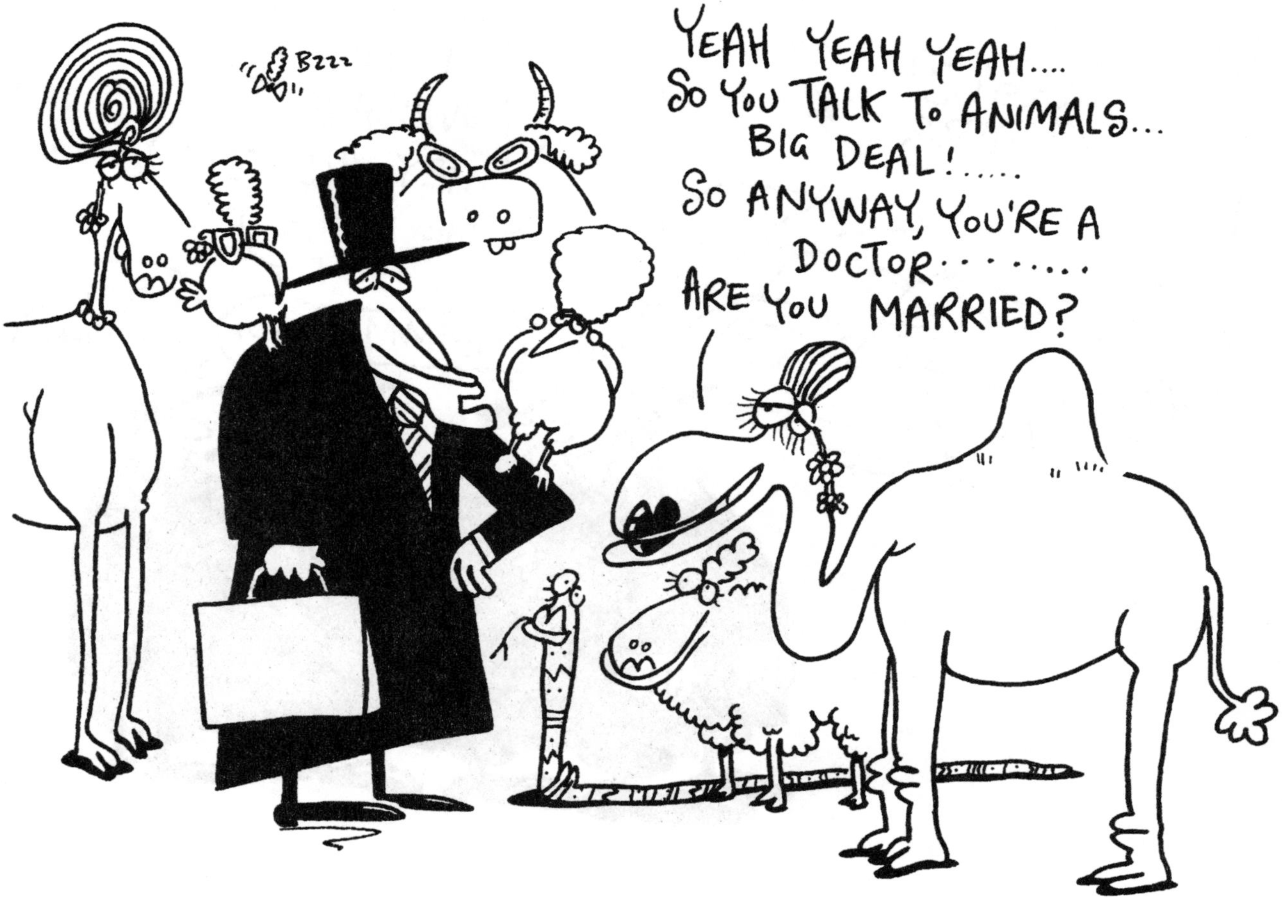
Bzzz
YEAH YEAH YEAH....
So YOU TALK TO ANIMALS...
BIG DEAL!.....
So ANYWAY, YOU'RE A
DOCTOR.........
ARE YOU MARRIED?

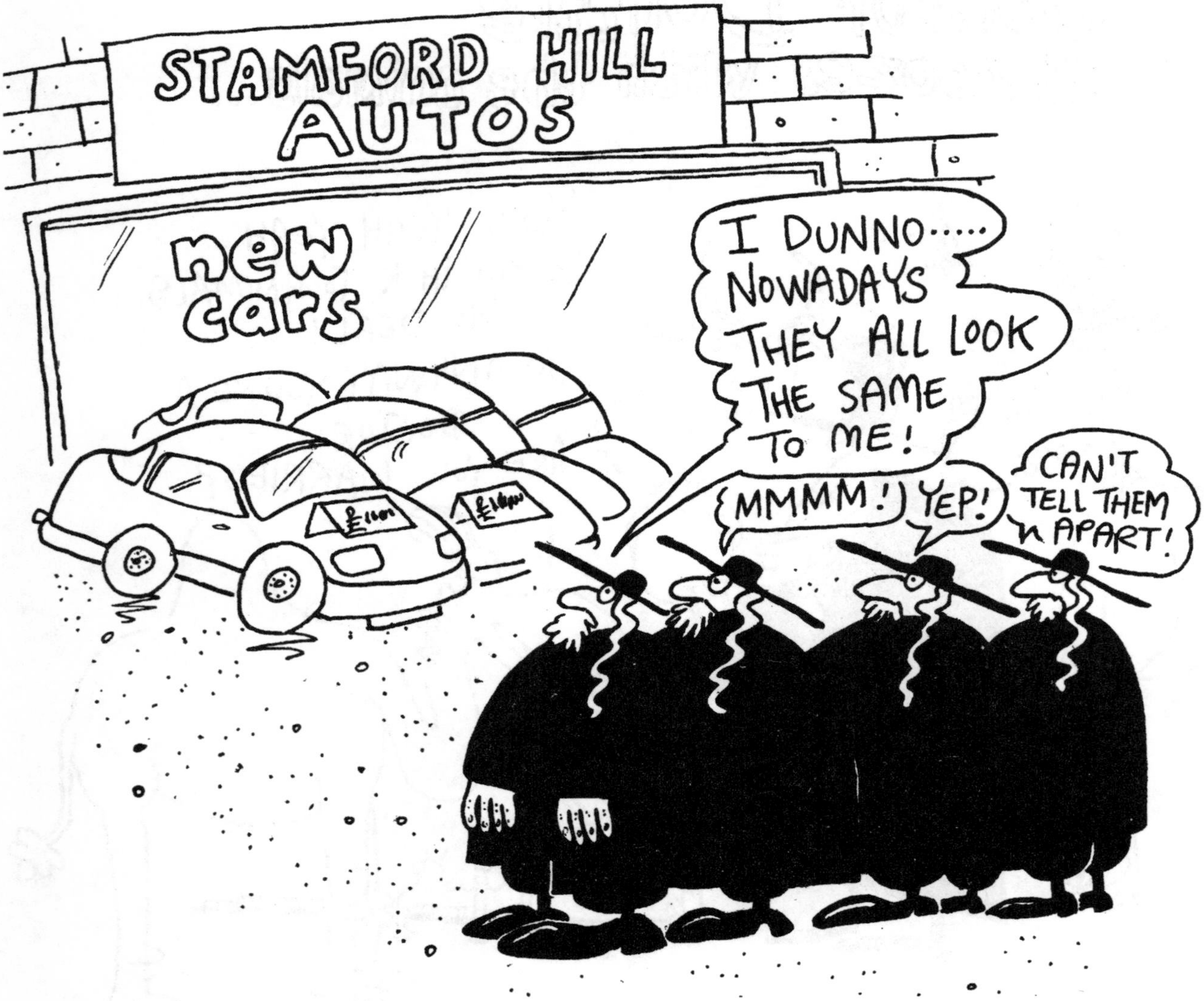
STAMFORD HILL AUTOS
new cars
I DUNNO..... NOWADAYS THEY ALL LOOK THE SAME TO ME!
MMMM!
YEP!
CAN'T TELL THEM APART!

THE CHOSEN FINAL EPISODE

And it came to pass that the Jewish people settled in the promised land, and built houses and cities and made the nation of Israel their home, despite being constantly at war with the aggressive neighbours.....

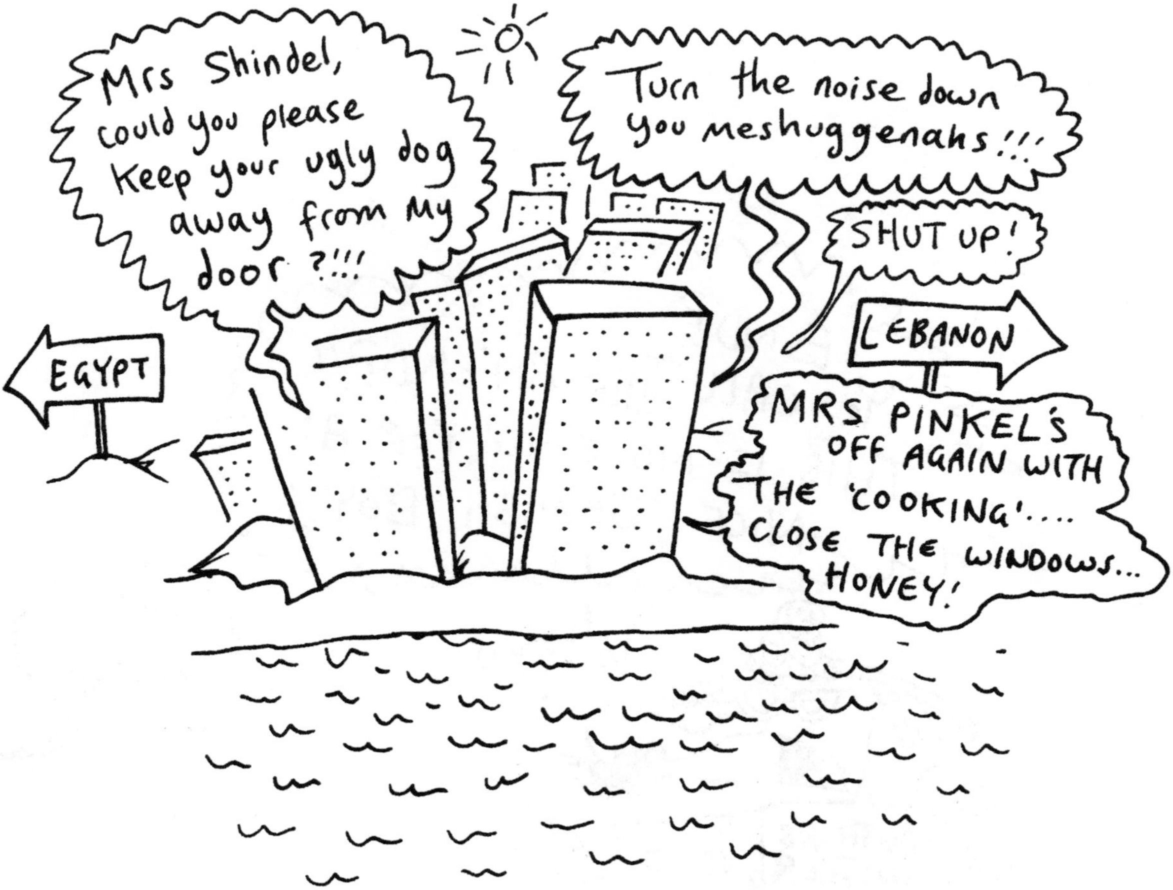
Mrs Shindel, could you please keep your ugly dog away from my door ?!!!
Turn the noise down you meshuggenahs!!!
SHUT UP!
EGYPT
LEBANON
MRS PINKEL'S OFF AGAIN WITH THE 'COOKING'.... CLOSE THE WINDOWS... HONEY!

THE END

END?
YOU CALL THIS AN 'END'?!!
......THIS IS NO 'END' FOR A NICE JEWISH BOY!!!
AUTHOR'S MOTHER
Sorry mother!